City Rider

This is going too far. The
anonymous rider making
his way through the rush-
hour traffic of Hyde Park
Corner gets full marks for
balance (note the
delicately outstretched
left hand and the brief-
case carefully parked
over the right shoulder)
and sang froid. But
smoking at the same time
. . . just who does he
think he is?

City Rider

How to survive with your bike

Nigel Thomas

Cartoons by Maddocks

ELM TREE BOOKS • London

First published in Great Britain 1981
by Elm Tree Books/Hamish Hamilton Ltd,
Garden House 57-59 Long Acre London WC2E 9JZ

Copyright © 1981 by Nigel Thomas
Cartoons copyright © 1981 by Maddocks

Book Design by Norman Reynolds

British Library Cataloguing in Publication Data

Thomas, Nigel
City rider.
1. Cycling
2. Urban transportation — Great Britain
I. Title
796.6'0941   GV1041
ISBN 0-241-10574-9
ISBN 0-241-10575-7 Pbk

Filmset by Pioneer
Printed in Hong Kong by
Wing King Tong Co. Ltd.

Contents

Acknowledgements

The author and publisher would like gratefully to acknowledge all those who gave their kind permission to reproduce copyright photographs in this book: Caroline Forbes, London Cycling Campaign, Richard Francis, Jay Myrdal, Keystone Press, Camera Press, Arthur Edwards, Press Association, Chris Barham, *Evening News*.

Chapter 1

On Your Bike

THIS book is intended to help the ordinary bike rider in town and city become a better cyclist. It is meant for the thousands who are now returning to pedal-power as a cheap, satisfying form of transport, not for competitive riders in their closed world of embrocation and agony. So better, in this book, means better than you were before not better than your neighbour. And better than you were before means safer and happier, not faster, fitter or more beautiful, which are simply by-products.

Happiness is important. It can be objectively shown in figures and tables that cycling is the cheapest, most convenient, most ecologically desirable form of personal transport in built-up areas, but such cold calculations are hardly inspiring in the frosty winter mornings. The appeal of cycling is that it is so enjoyable. It soaks away the frustrations and tensions of other ways of travelling so that you are more cheerful after a ride, even through the rush hour. Happiness can be easily spoiled, and undoubtedly its greatest destroyer is fear.

The first thing a non-cyclist says to you is: 'But isn't it terribly dangerous?' It would be foolish to deny the menace of sharing the carriageway with motor vehicles and, on the face of it, cycling does turn up at the alarming end of the accident statistics. But although it is more often the other party to blame when an accident involves a cyclist — say the police — the answer lies in your own hands. It is possible to ride in such a way as to minimise the risks. It's worth the effort since it's so obviously good for your peace of mind.

The second most common bar to a sense of harmony is failing to match yourself to your machine. Keeping warm (but not too sweaty), keeping dry, keeping clean, all involve techniques we've used in our roles as pedestrians, office or factory workers, even motorists. New techniques are needed for the new role of cyclist. Again, smoothing away such small irritations brings disproportionate benefits to your state of mind.

The third requirement is a certain minimum of mechanical nous. The bicycle is a machine for which you are responsible. It's a personal choice whether you wish to enmesh yourself in the mysteries of ball-bearing races and tangential spoking, but you shouldn't run a bike unless you're willing to keep it lubricated, its nuts and bolts tightened and its tyres inflated, just the same as you shouldn't run anything electrical at home unless you're going to keep the wires, plugs and fuses safe.

In the golden age that never was, all the necessary bits of knowledge and experience were passed down the generations by parent and grandparent, along with the heavyweight, repainted First Grown-Up Bike, with its symbolic new bell. Unfortunately the Fifties, Sixties and Seventies — when for a form of transport to be cheap, efficient, harmless and pleasant to use condemned it as hopelessly old-fashioned — have ruptured this fragile chain of expertise. This book, by a combination of personal trial-and-error (often collected with a blushing face from professional mechanics), the experience of friends and acquaintances, and a certain amount of paper research, will try to pass on some of the hard-won tricks and information that may have skipped a generation.

Most of all, though, there are problems that modern urban cyclists particularly face. These include clothing, not just what you wear when riding, but also what you find yourself standing up in when you reach your destination, load carrying, security and safe riding in a traffic-bound city that is only just beginning to be reclaimed, by pedestrians as well, from the car. A new tradition is beginning to grow which covers all these things.

Getting one's first real bicycle was an important step for a child, the first present that was neither a toy nor as tediously useful as a jumper or a new satchel. It meant independence. The freedom to visit people and places away from home. The right to stay or to go on your own whim, not anyone else's. Also, of course, it was a grown-up machine. People went to work or off courting on it. Rounds were done, visits made and things collected.

All this was before the motor car usurped the bicycle's role of liberator. Nowadays serious business is only done to the background noise of machinery and the smell of burning petrol. Pedal power was only good enough for cranky nuts or paupers or, of course, women and children, and that strange no-longer-one thing, not-yet-another body the university students.

The world of the bicycle split into two. On the one hand were earnest healthy types who spent their time measuring the clearance between their wheels and their frame in thicknesses of cigarette paper, and broke the pain barrier twice before breakfast. On the other, the utility riders whose machines were expected to squeak their way unminded from one rusty winter to the next in much the same way as the aged retainer in horror films hobbles along the corridors.

If the rickshaw was good enough for Imperialist hyenas . . . seriously, no strap on two-year-old Duncan and a flapping trouser leg show the picture was posed. The stability of a trike, when ridden at moderate pace, *makes for worry-free child transport.*

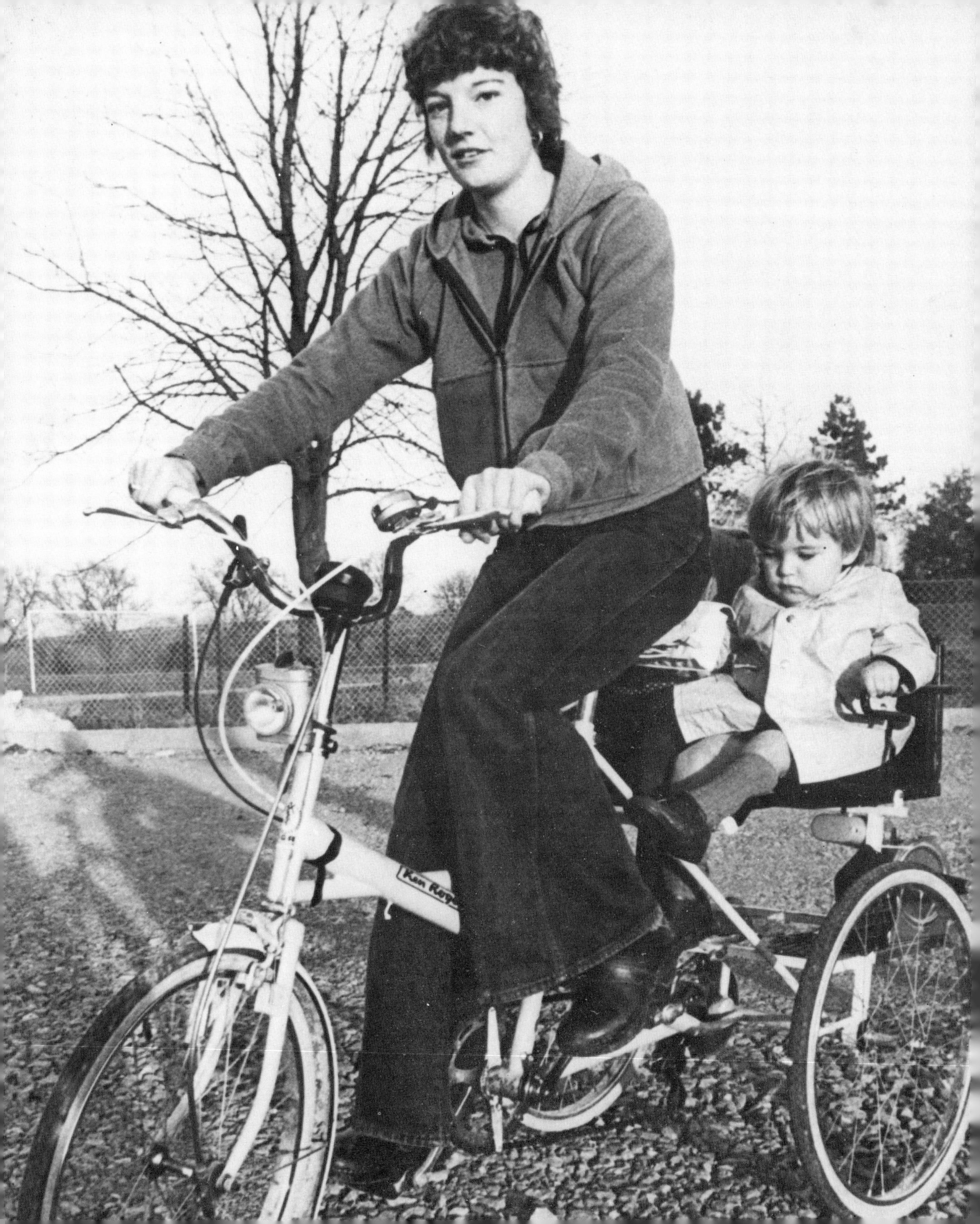

But there is a middle way, and its time at last has come. The car, after years of dominating the collective imagination, is in economic and environmental disgrace. Riding a bike allows you to bask in all the Puritan virtues: thrift, social responsibility, health and humility. Cycling, like brown bread, is incontestably a good thing. And, like brown bread, it can be made out to be some sort of worthy self-denial. Virtuous maybe, but no fun. This is a guilt-ridden lie. Real whole-grain bread doesn't have to dry the palate and clog the jaw, it can taste like cake. Cycling too makes a pleasure out of a necessity. The truth of this is proved every time you ride past two or three million pounds worth of steaming and deteriorating machinery filled with steaming and deteriorating people all trying, as you are succeeding, to get to work. And you hear the birds sing and feel the sun and the wind in your hair. It is the only form of medium range land transport which can deposit you at your destination glowing not just with the flush of exercise but also with a silly grin of pure happiness. If a conspiracy of machine, traffic, clothing and your own attitude is allowed to take away this pleasure, you have been robbed blind.

The Machine

The worst mistake you can make is to equip yourself with the wrong kind of bike; wrong for you and your purposes that is. Although the manufacturers of small-wheeled folding bikes have been known to place professional racing cyclists on their curious machines this does not prove, as they would like to imply, that the respectable times produced in this way show the small-wheeler to be almost as good a way of covering ground as any other bike. Leaving aside your longing to do wheelies round the dustbins on the shopping precinct (and this is usually pretty well suppressed by your late teens), any advantages the small-wheeler has are unconnected with what it feels like to ride, which is essentially unstable. They are, rather unconvincingly, the alleged ease of carrying shopping and greater convenience of storage.

Leaving these aside then, there are four basic categories from which to choose: the racing bike, the sports bike, what they like to call a commuter bike and the roadster. On the whole these are in descending order of price and delicacy of adjustment, and in ascending order of weight and effort. The mechanical differences between them are set out in the next chapter, together with the consequences for the rider. Your first step, though, is to determine what you want a bike for.

If you're thinking of buying a racing bike then you presumably know something about the subject and have a fair idea of what sort of racing you want to do and the right machine to do it on. If you don't, or if you fancy looking flash outside the swimming baths on Saturday afternoons, then you've got more money than sense and should take the consequences. One thing to watch, though, is that most big manufacturers produce a model which looks just like a racing bike but isn't. If the gleaming confection you're ogling in the shop costs much under £200 then this is what it is. It may well be very good value but it is intended for teenagers and, unless you are one, you should beware the temptations.

Sports bikes are becoming the fastest-selling category of adult machines and they cover the widest range. At the top they are made with the same lightweight and expensive materials as a racing bike, and with the same care. Small differences in design and fittings mark them out as intended for long-distance leisure riding, rather than racing, and they are often called tourers instead of sports. As the price comes down so does the quality of the components, but it has to sink a long way before the bike is not worth buying. As always, though, there is a point beyond which the bike will become so irritating to ride and awkward to maintain that it just isn't worth it, even at the price. At the moment, if you can't afford more than about £120 then you should lower your sights a category.

A sports bike will generally have drop handle-bars, ten-speed — sometimes five — derailleur gears (the ones with the mechanism exposed and an arm extending below the rear cluster to carry the chain), metal rat-trap pedals able to take toe-clips and 27-inch wheels with 1¼-inch rims or narrower, capable of taking high-pressure tyres. It should be possible to fit mudguards and luggage carriers.

This is the sort of bike for those who want to ride either fast, or over long distances. It doesn't do this by itself, of course, and the new owner of a gleaming ten-speed should beware of feeling humiliated or, even worse, challenged by the character on a battered old clunker who sideslips through the traffic ahead of him making a sound like a cat's torture chamber and waggling a rusty mudguard like a duck's tail. In this form of transport the rider still counts for more than the steed. Personally you will find that improved manoeuverability, acceleration and braking will enable you to thread the traffic jams with greater comfort and confidence, faster and more safely. As for riding any distance, you have to be very fit and determined to ride a heavy roadster for fifty miles without getting tired to the point of misery. On a middle-priced sports lightweight, anybody can do it.

After the sports bike comes a rather strange hybrid, the commuter bike. It's hard to say whether it's a sports bike with flat handlebars or a roadster with derailleur gears (usually five). Probably the latter. This is a not unreasonable compromise provided you're sure that you won't want to extend your cycling activities much further than the journey to work or down to the shops.

The roadster is basic bike. It's defining characteristics are usually a wide mattress saddle, strong thick tyres with wide rims, flat handlebars, and, if it has gears at all, the three-speed type with the mechanism hidden away from sight and screwdriver in the rear-wheel hub. Heavy and relatively slow it may be, but do not underestimate this vehicle. It is the most common form of mechanical transport in the world. Economies are dependent on it and wars have been won by it. It has been ridden through jungles and over mountains, and even all the way round the world. I would never suggest that you should neglect to oil it and tighten its nuts and bolts, drop it casually to the ground or leave it out in the rain, but even if this is how you

behave the machine is likely to repay you by taking you cheaply, comfortably and reliably wherever you want to go for years.

As always there are various grades within the category and usually you get what you pay for, but in this case more expensive is likely to mean stronger and more reliable, rather than lighter. It makes sense to choose one of the well-known makes. A reputation for trustworthiness which extends to all five continents, like Raleigh's, is not thrown away casually.

In Third World countries, America and dramatically in Holland, the standard roadster has shallow frame angles and long raked front forks which give a soft wallowy sort of ride, but makes for comfort and stability over rough tracks and paths, and the Amsterdam cobbles. Ironically the Americans refer to our sort of bike, which is designed on the assumption of at least tolerably macadammed roads, as an English racer. It's a misleading name by modern standards, but the respect it embodies is well deserved.

Despite the tolerance with which the roadster responds to neglect, it makes sense to look after any bike. Total neglect of a highly tuned sports bike will make it noticeably more uncomfortable to ride quite quickly, other bikes may gently decline for years without you being any the wiser although the effects are still felt in the body. A vague feeling of dissatisfaction could be the result of handlebars out of true, which force you to ride with your back slightly twisted, or bent cranks which disturb the smooth movement of your legs, or perhaps a loose headset which makes the steering judder. You may not realise that something is wrong and even when you do it can be hard to decide exactly what, but somewhere a faint but persistent alarm bell is ringing, telling the back of your brain that this journey is lurching perilously on the edge of disaster. When you get off you decide to travel some other way next time.

Of the more than 14 million bikes there are estimated to be in Britain, a good guess says that perhaps 5 million are rarely used. These black-and-rust tangles cluttering up the shed or the cupboard under the stairs can probably be coaxed

a few miles, given a puff or two of air for the tyres, but the experience will be so horrible it could put you off for life. It only requires a little care, say ten minutes a month for a bike in regular use, and your bike will never sink into this lumpenlimbo and will continue to deliver all the joys and satisfactions of walking — at half the effort and three times the speed.

The Bickerton in action. Truly portable (it goes as hand-luggage on the train), very well made and expensive to buy, and with a gentlemanly wobble as you ride, this bike is obviously the perfect executive commuter machine. Look at that dignified passing of the bus.

Here are three simple rules for buying a bike:

1. Always buy the best you can afford. Inevitably there has to be a compromise between what you would like ideally and economic reality, but aim as high as you can and you will get the benefit not only when you ride but also if you wanted to sell. Well-made bikes keep their value very well. And don't forget to include in your calculations the fact that you'll begin saving money on fares and petrol the moment you leave the shop.

2. Get the best frame for your money that you can. Cheap brakes, wheels or gears can be easily upgraded, but the frame sets the upper limit on any transformation. A three-speed frame can only be converted to take derailleur five or ten speed gears with great difficulty, and the attempt is never quite satisfactory.

13

You should make allowance for the possibility that your cycling ambitions will grow with practice. When you begin, the four-mile trot to work may be the most you dream of, but after a few months a Sunday ride into the country begins to look more and more desirable. The best thing is to buy a bike just a little bit better than you think you'll need, and then grow into it. Otherwise, try and get a model that can be improved. Remember a roadster, however magnificent, can never really be anything more.

3. The Fit is vital. Handlebars and seat height can be adjusted but you must get the right size frame. On the whole the principle is to get the largest size you can manage. Frame sizes are measured in inches and are taken from the length of the seat tube, measured from the centre of the join with the crossbar to the centre of the bottom bracket shell. The usual adult range is from 21 inches to 25 inches, though extreme sizes outside this span can be found. There are various formulae: a man of 5' 8'' should look first at a 22½ inch frame for instance, a woman of 5' 6'' should begin at 21 inches. Some people say you should deduct four inches from your inside leg measurement. The basic principle, though, is that you should be able to straddle the crossbar with both feet comfortably flat on the ground. However bodies vary in shape and relative proportion as well as size, and it's best to find someone experienced, either a friend or a cycle dealer, and straddle a few machines of varying size in front of them to get their opinion. If it has no crossbar, use a straight stick to make a temporary one to measure from.

Ladies and Gents

The open or step-through frame, which does without a crossbar, is usually called a ladies frame. It is inherently weaker than the conventional diamond frame and distributes its properties of rigidity and resilience less well. In order to counteract its geometrical weakness, it is usually made with heavier gauge tubing and therefore weighs more.

There is absolutely no anatomical reason for a woman to ride a bike without a crossbar. Indeed, a traumatic unseating which dumped you suddenly on the crossbar could well be more unpleasant for a man. The advantage that such a frame does have is that it can be mounted without swinging the leg high, and for this reason such a frame is often used by people with a physical reason to avoid such a movement — for instance, because of an artificial hip. It's also true that, although most skirts can be worn while riding with a crossbar, the 'ladies frame' is rather more convenient. Long skirts still run the risk of getting tangled up in the chainwheel or brake blocks, of course, but with an about-town roadster, bike chain and spoke guards can be fitted.

As far as lighter bikes and longer distances are concerned, the suspicion remains that the ladies frame is a tribute to little womanism, the unspoken belief that a woman is too nervous to ride a bike with a crossbar and that it is vaguely indecent for her to raise a leg above her hip to mount the bike. However, not all cycle dealers these days are quite so quick to steer a woman customer away from an ordinary bike.

Holland: is it advice or invitation?

Colour

Part of the pleasure of owning a nice bike is that it looks good. Some people may try to make you feel frivolous and silly if you confess that the colour of your bike matters to you. Let them stew in their grey austerity. Flashing down the street in the sunlight on the colour of your choice is one of the pleasures of life. It feels even better if you've just washed your hair and are wearing a clean, favourite shirt. Unfortunately, most middle-priced models come in only one or two colours. If you can't stand them, this really is a good reason for looking elsewhere. Almost every model has a nearly exact equivalent in another manufacturer's range. I know of one adequate but mechanically unspectacular bike that's sold phenomenally well on the strength of its pretty shade of pink.

Traffic

One thing that's likely to postpone indefinitely a decision to pedal into work, is a perfectly natural reluctance to join in the lethal game of dodgems that is played between the pavements in all towns and cities. They, after all, are armoured against the consequences of their recklessness in expensively designed metal boxes, and gamble only their garage bills and no-claims bonuses against the outcome (or so they think). We deal in elbows, heads, skin and blood. On the face of it, a cruel mismatch. The figures would seem to show the inevitable consequence: cycling is ten times more dangerous than travelling in a car, according to a government report a few years ago. It's small consolation that the cyclist is usually not at fault in the accident.

Like all statistics, though, these claims need to be approached with scepticism. For numerate game players there is a fascinating argument to join about whether accidents per mile, accidents per journey or accidents per year is the proper measure. If you take the last, then the sum works out as a motorist being likely to suffer only half as many accidents per year as a cyclist.

These are grim thoughts from which to try and draw comfort. I have no desire to go to work every morning relying on the odds of getting there in one piece resolving into an acceptable risk. The next thought is grimmer still. About half the cyclist victims of accidents are children, and a ten- to fourteen-year-old is seven times as likely to appear in the figures as someone in their twenties. Motorists, of course, are all adults, though not many behave like it. What it means is that adult cyclists have a much better chance of a safe ride than the figures seem to show at first. There is another lesson to be drawn from this slaughter of the innocents. It is because they are children that they suffer so disproportionately. They are more careless, more impulsive, more trusting. A cyclist who ruthlessly eliminates these qualities is well on the way to eliminating the risks.

The way to conquer fear is to cycle fearfully. Assume that every car and van is driven by a person of slow mind and slower reflexes. That they can barely grasp the difference between brake and accelerator, have left their powerful spectacles at home and are, moreover, motivated by a sullen malevolence against everyone who is not driving a car.

You should cycle so as to leave this monster a sufficient margin to do his worst without harming you.

Surprisingly this intense wariness quickly becomes a habit which requires no thought so, with your mind freed of the monkey of fear, you can concentrate on enjoying the ride.

Clothing

Discomfort kills pleasure. If you persist in the town-dweller's obstinate refusal to suit what they wear to the weather and the activity, you will be uncomfortable and irritable. Cycling is an outdoor exercise and demands a certain minimum of concessions both to the climate and to the exercise. If you ride in a heavy suit you will get hot and bothered; in tight clothes, sore and stiff; in delicate pale clothes, dirty and upset. It's a small matter to think about the suitability of what you're about to dress yourself in, and once it's done right you can forget it.

Attitude

There's no denying that bicycling requires a certain amount of effort and concentration. It is not a passive activity and doesn't fit well with the idea that certain things we have to do, like getting to work each morning, are holes in the day, good for nothing except gentle thought. You cannot expect to get on a bike as you do a bus or a train, without giving it a moment's thought before or after, and drift through your journey half asleep.

On the other hand, there's nothing more off-putting than zealous self-improvement in a cyclist. Seek the Middle Way. It is worth bothering to learn certain techniques because for most people they work. It becomes easier to use your bike, you have to think about it less and, after a while, cycling becomes as natural as walking and you can concentrate on the sunshine or the scenery. You can take the learning too far, though, until it takes up so much thought and worry that cycling no longer counts as a useful everyday skill and becomes a hobby — and that is another thing entirely. When it gets out of control you end up with people who nervously introduce themselves by their pedalling cadence. 'Hi, I do 72. I was 68 until last year.' The sad consequences of this attitude are summed up in a letter I once saw in an American magazine: 'I've been cycling thirty miles a day for the past four years, but last month I read your article by Dr —, and I found I've been pedalling wrong!'

The mistake here is to treat ordinary cycling as if it were a sport. It may certainly be reasonable for sporting riders to change something they have been doing for years on the advice of a coach, but they're trying to cut fractions of a second off their times. We don't have to copy the fanatical fitness of the racers in order to learn from them. But we're not after the same perfection either. Most of the new equipment is derived from the improvements to racing bikes, and certainly their skills are applicable to all sorts of riding since nobody willingly wastes effort when they're racing. The difference is not in what they do, but in the fact that they have to do it until it hurts, and that's not a desirable characteristic of a form of transport.

Chapter 2

The Dream Machine

MORE than half the 1.5 million bikes sold in Britain each year are bought by adults and, when you're trying to work out which one is best for you, it sometimes seems as if every one was different. This apparent complexity isn't a conspiracy by elitist club riders to exclude you from the inner circle, nor, come to that, a plot by the manufacturers to rifle your wallet (well, not much of a one anyway), it's the direct consequence of the nature of the machine.

A bicycle is not a single designed unit — it is a collection of parts, mostly manufactured by different specialist firms, which can be put together in any number of combinations to provide just the riding characteristics you want. The true obsessive dreams endlessly of teaming a different rim with a new spoke, lost in rapt contemplation of the minute difference this might make to his ride. Worse still he will talk about it endlessly. It may be boring, but it is quite harmless. It is also quite unnecessary. The principles of bicycle design are fairly simple to grasp, and from there you simply work out what you want your bicycle to do. If you take that answer, along with a good idea of what you want to pay, to any decent bicycle shop you can happily leave the experts to fill in the brand names. What follows is a basic outline of what makes one bike different from another, and how the differences affect the rider.

It is generally agreed that the fundamental characteristics of the modern bicycle are the diamond frame with a chain driven back wheel — the so-called Safety bicycle which evolved from James Starley's designs of the 1880s — and the pneumatic tyre which was developed at the end of that decade by Belfast's most celebrated vet, James Boyd Dunlop. Since then the history of the bicycle has been mainly of steady improvement of parts and balance, while the governing principles of design have barely changed. For a time it was even claimed that the bicycle was humanity's only complex tool which had actually been developed to the point of perfection. Perfectly ludicrous, of course, but anybody who has ever ridden down an English lane on a hot August day with their bicycle in a peak of adjustment can only sympathise with such excessive enthusiasm.

The bicycle is going through another period of creative imagination at the moment, spurred on by the general rediscovery of its advantages as a system of basic individual transport, but for some years the basic diamond-framed safety design, which is just coming up to its centenary, is going to hog the road. The most likely area of fundamental change is in lowering wind resistance, the thing that absorbs most of the rider's energy, either by some sort of streamlining or by completely altering the riding position. By a combination of both measures, experimentalist riders have managed to push the unpaced speed record to over 60 mph, and in America a magnificent eccentric, Captain Dan Henry, has been the guiding light of a more everyday design of recumbent bike. It does work, but most people find the low position too nerve-racking in traffic, and too unnatural for sustained effort, for this to be a serious challenge to tradition, at the moment anyway.

Surely, the observant will point out, this ignores the fundamental change in the bikes you see on the roads. The revolution is not some way off in the future but began back in the early sixties when Alex Moulton introduced his small-wheeled design.

A good Dutch sense of priorities.

Now you see small-wheelers everywhere and they've pretty well taken over the discount, special offer, department store market. Here we are entering an area of murky controversy, but in my opinion the small-wheeler was not an advance but a backward step. They are not so nice to ride and, with one important exception which I'll come to, they don't deliver any of the advantages claimed for them. They are a typical product of the decade that spawned them — all image. It was a brilliant marketing move.

The sixties were the low point in the story of the bicycle. Car ownership was booming and the key words were newness and fun. Bikes were either for children, or for pedalling through the grey gates of some Northern mill to work in a dying industry, or they were sporting equipment. Although sales never sunk as far as you might have thought, the bicycle was definitely Out. Then came the Moulton. It looked different, exciting, it had the whiff of modernity; with it came unlikely tales of Fun People carrying bikes in the boots of their magnolia Rolls Royces. The small-wheel bike folds up, so flat dwellers could store it easily out of the way. The small-wheeler was a false dawn, but all the brouhaha did achieve something. First, the small-wheeler was sold as a city bike, and, although it's not ideal for the purpose, it did help to start the growing awareness that the bicycle is the best means of personal transport around town yet devised. Second, what with a Lord Chancellor and a six-foot-seven MP being photographed pedalling round Parliament Square, and actresses chaining up their steeds outside Chelsea restaurants, the mini boom began the process of rehabilitating the lumpen grey-flannel image of cycling for adults. I hope the craze is dying now, but a quick look at what is wrong with the design is as good a way as any of showing what a city rider's machine should be.

One of the things that always surprises me is the claim that the low centre of gravity of the small-wheeler is an advantage. Although there is less machinery high in the air, there is not much that can be done with the shape of the human body. And the centre of gravity of machine and rider is far too high in relation to the axles. It may sound like a technical matter, but you can feel the difference. On a full-sized bike, the point of balance of bike and rider is somewhere around the seat, and that is exactly the plane of your two points of pivot when riding — the handlebars and your bottom — so you feel part of the machine, it bends and balances naturally. On a small-wheeler, every-thing feels underneath you, as if you had stepped on a roller-skate, and balancing becomes an effort — even if you are aware of nothing more than the mildest insecurity. The consequences for the rider are two. First, you always consciously steer a small-

wheeler, whereas, on a full-sizer, it seems to change direction automatically as your thoughts direct. The second, is that you wobble more on the small-wheeler, and wobbling in town traffic is a fatal vice — perhaps literally.

Wobbling is partly a nervous reaction to the roller-skate effect of those little wheels spinning away somewhere down at ankle height, and it is partly a direct consequence of the frame design. The diamond frame is based on triangles which derive their strength from their geometry not the bulk of metal in the members. Triangles work by transmitting stress forces equally throughout the geometric system they are part of. If you sit the bike properly, holding the bars firmly without clutching at them, weight distributed between feet, hands and bottom in a proportion something like 2:1:1, your body joins in with the triangulation, arms, back and crossbar topping off the structure. Only your head, heavy though that is, remains outside the system, which distributes road shock and cornering stresses throughout all its parts and thus absorbs them smoothly.

The small-wheeled bike in effect carries its weight on the end of a strong pole which is fixed only at one end. Naturally, with such leverage, the weight is going to wave about. Not all that much, maybe, but the body notices it and tries to correct. The result is wobble, as well as whitened knuckles and a vague but permanent sense of unease.

Because they lack geometric strength, small-wheelers have to compensate with stronger members, so on the whole they are relatively heavy — certainly heavier than the equivalent quality large-wheeler. And, to make matters worse, they are

OVERLEAF: *This mob is about to set off on a London-to-Brighton run. The organisers claimed 'it was not a pedal-power demonstration'. Note the division of labour: the strongest rider carries everybody's lights.*

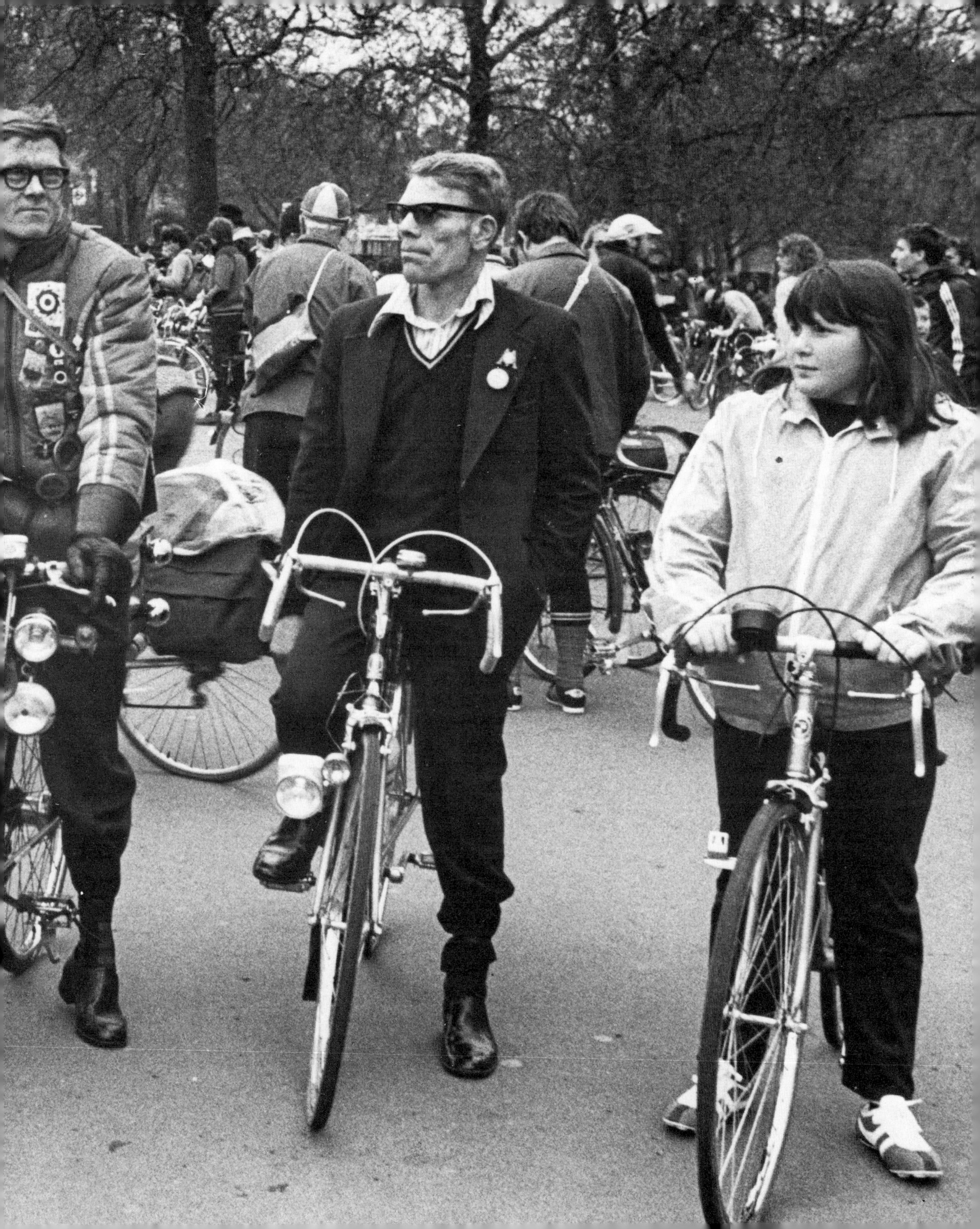

always harder work to pedal because the rolling resistance of a small wheel is much greater than a large one.

The problem doesn't end there. Small wheels will obviously fail to smooth out the bumps in a road surface as well as a large diameter wheel. The bigger diameter can literally bridge a 2-foot ravine without noticing, whereas the smaller curvature rim will sink perceptibly in, and jolt perceptibly out. To compound the problem, the short spokes make a small wheel far more rigid than the large one, so more of the road shock is transmitted up into the rider's body. Alex Moulton knew this when he introduced his design, and in fact his most significant innovation was the use of a sprung suspension system to absorb the punishment. By one of the great ironies of technological history, this aspect of his design has been completely abandoned, and manufacturers have chosen instead to fit fat bulgy tyres, which certainly soak up the bumps, but whose rolling resistance is so horrific that cycling becomes like walking through a swamp.

I'm sure it is because no-one in full possession of the facts would want to use a small-wheeler to travel across country that the design has been characterised as suitable for towns. For some reason trips through built-up areas are thought of as always being short. Foldability is mainly a red herring. With the exception of the highly-prized (and highly-priced) Bickerton model, most designs are simply changed from an awkward but familiar shape, into an equally awkward confusion in which something always sticks out in the wrong place. I have never met anybody who actually folded up their folder after each journey and hid it away in a cupboard. In the same way, the manoeuverability in traffic that was claimed, is the inspired dream of someone safely wedded to their car. If I had to choose one quality that is most essential for safe riding in towns, it must be the ability to keep to a straight unwavering line — any bike is quite nippy enough for the zig zagging between bonnet and boot which car drivers jealously, and quite incorrectly, believe is the secret of our advantage in traffic.

The chopper in all its lurid, metalflake variations, has captured the hearts and minds of most children, particularly in the towns. Any bike is better than none, but it is painful to watch. First, these machines have been designed to look as much like motorbikes as possible. Heavy studded tyres, front mudguards that imply a long travel front suspension, banana seats, stick gear shifts; the only thing a real cyclist could approve is the large rear reflector.

The Americans call them cafe racers, and they're designed to look flash, with the weight back over the rear wheel — just perfect for the 300-yard sprint to the Wimpy bar, finishing off with a wheelie over the curb and an awe-inspiring skid-stop at the end. In the country, however, where schoolfriends can live five or ten miles away and they whisper nostalgically about local bus services in the Darby and Joan club, the bike is still the great liberator — first steps on the road to self-determination — and the choppers never really caught on. Some designs are truly horrific, death traps of folded tin, weak frame and insufficient bearings. Others are responsibly made, as safe as the basic limitations of the design allow, and would be fine if they were only used for hanging out after school. Unfortunately, they're taken on to busy roads as well, where not only does their poor handling in traffic make accidents more likely, but clunky gear levers and redundant accessories can spoil what would otherwise have been a lucky escape with horrible rips and tears.

Off the road it's a different matter. No reasonable parent can object to their children bumping into hard ground now and again; hard travelling radiators are another matter. In the blossoming sport of BMX, or bicycle motor-cross, the faults of the cafe racer become virtues. These are short dirt-track sprints, with many bends and dips and bumps. Style here is a matter of defeating the laws of probability. To come out of a corner back wheel first, at an angle of 45°, with the front axle level with your nose, is called being radical — a word of high praise. BMX bikes have descended from the cafe racer, but they're more strongly built and they've begun to rediscover the secret of elegant bicycle design; on the whole they're made to suit a purpose. Apart from being tremendous fun, there's no doubt your bicycle handling improves radically as well.

The second, and greatest, virtue of the small-wheeler is its adaptability. In almost all models, seat and handlebars can be raised or lowered so much that all sizes of person, from the child who has just learnt to ride upwards, can ride the same machine. If you just want one bike in the household, this selling-point is unanswerable. The diamond frame cannot compete.

The parts of the frame

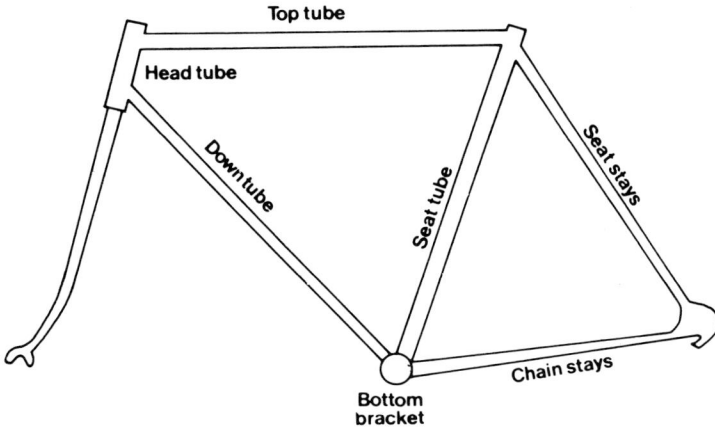

Top tube

Head tube

Down tube

Seat tube

Seat stays

Chain stays

Bottom bracket

Typical dimensions

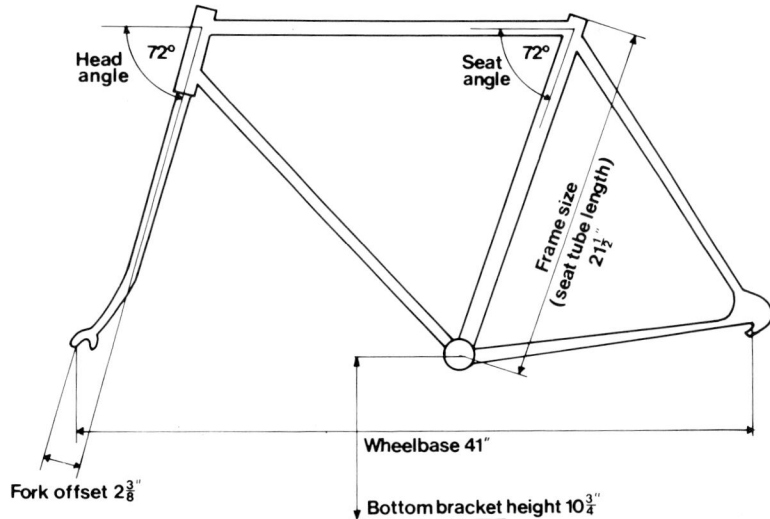

Head angle 72°

Seat angle 72°

Frame size (seat tube length) 21½"

Wheelbase 41"

Fork offset 2⅜"

Bottom bracket height 10¾"

Diagrams courtesy of TI Raleigh

The diagrams overleaf show the basic shape of the bicycle. If you want a serious form of transport around town your machine will look like this. There are various adjustments you can make to the proportions which will, for instance, give you a faster, more responsive and less comfortable ride.

The size of a frame is given (in inches in Britain) by the length of the seat tube (see fig 2). It's important to get this right and to adjust the seat, bars and brake levers to suit yourself. There are some impressive mathematical ways of doing this (do you know the length of your femur in millimetres?) but a simple and quite effective combination of rule of thumb and trial and error is described in chapter 5.

The quality and the characteristics of a bicycle are determined by the materials and the proportions of the frame. At root two conflicting tendencies have to be reconciled. A stiff unyielding frame transforms the greater proportion of your pedalling power into forward motion, while more relaxed angles give a smoother ride and iron out jerky steering as well as uneven roads. Taken to either extreme, the bike becomes impractical but where the balance is struck depends on what the bike is to be used for.

A bicycle frame is designated by its seat angle (see diagram) which in the most common 'parallel' configuration is the same as the head angle. The higher the number the stiffer and more nervous the ride. 72° is common on touring bikes, 73° might suit a hard-riding tourist, and 74° or above would only be found on pure racing machines. Similarly, shortening the wheelbase by reducing the offset on the front forks and reducing the length of the chain stays, also contributes to a hard, whippy ride. Beware though, this process can mean that there is not enough clearance for mudguards, and lead to something called overlap. This means that the front wheel bangs into the toeclips if turned too far and is common on racing bikes though undesirable in general. It is also illegal in America.

The problem of suspension exercised the minds of bike designers long before Alex Moulton and his small-wheeled frame. Spoked wheels absorb much of the road shock, and the longer the spokes the more effectively they do it, which is why the penny farthing was rideable at all. However, the significant development was the air-filled tyre. Jarring is not only uncomfortable but it also slows you down enormously. Since all the energy in a moving bicycle is supplied by the rider, an efficient engine but of extremely low output, any waste is immediately noticeable. And the rider must supply the effort for the bike to bounce up and down as well as for forward motion. It is astonishingly apparent how much speed you lose when the bike hits a rough patch of road. So efficient a solution is the pneumatic tyre that when it made its first appearance, on a Belfast racetrack in 1888, the rider W. Hume easily outstripped all the other competitors. Nowadays tyres are pumped up hard, to pressures between 60 and 120 lbs per square inch, as this cuts down the energy wasted in flexing the walls of the tyre. But this is a matter of degree, the pneumatic tyre remains the bicycle's secret weapon.

The spoked wheel is a vital part of the bicycle's development. It is light, strong, and an efficient absorber of jarring and bouncing. The normal size of a wheel is 27-inch diameter (or 700C continental size), but some old-fashioned shallow-angled frames take a 28-inch wheel with big balloon tyres, and 26-inch wheels are also found. (Since the wheel is constant, some small-frame sizes look rather out of proportion, and manufacturers have begun making quite good quality bikes with smaller wheels. This enables a child to ride a 'proper' bike even when quite small, and is worth considering if you happen to be a short adult.)

Fully set up for touring, with loaded panniers, britches and natty white socks. This rider is trying too hard to look as if he knew what he was doing. In fact the bike-load is mainly packed lunch and two bottles of wine, and they're talking about whether it would be a good idea to write a bike book.

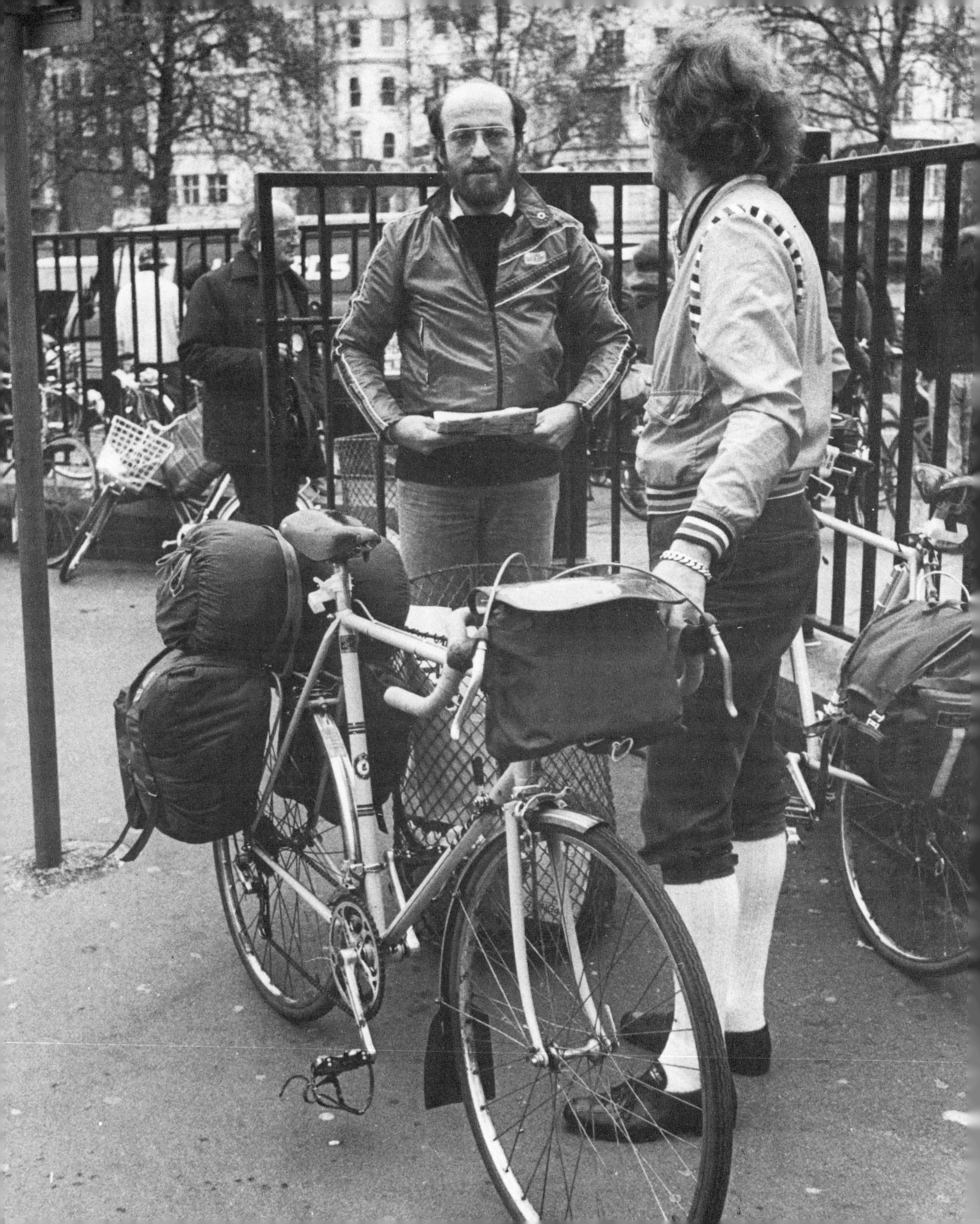

A wheel is a masterpiece of balanced forces. From a hub less than 3 inches wide, a thin rim of metal is laced into a circle with wire spokes. Although it seems fragile, the structure is very strong, but this depends on keeping the right tension on the spokes. If you have one broken, missing or loose, it will put extra strain on the others.

Hubs vary in quality and price from relatively simple tubes of steel holding two ball-bearing races, to finely machined alloy works of art with a price to match. Hubs are equipped with 28, 32, 36 or 40 spokeholes — generally speaking the more spokes the greater strength — and there are different patterns of lacing that can be used; but these are arcane matters, best left to the wheel-builder. For general riding in town simply ask for a touring wheel, which is designed for strength and resilience.

There are three main categories of wheel, but unfortunately a minefield of subdivisions inside them. The chief trap these set for the unwary are in replacement tyres. It's only too easy to buy a tyre that doesn't quite fit. Until you are familiar with the options, always take the wheel with you to the shop when buying a tyre.

The first two categories of wheel are 'wire-ons'. In cross section these tyres are horseshoe-shaped, with a wire bead at the open edge which grips the rim when the inner tube is inflated. Unless you are getting very serious about performance, yours will be one of these. The basic balloon tyre fits on to a 1½-inch rim, is heavy with rubber (and therefore very durable) and is inflated to relatively low pressures. The High Pressure tyre traditionally fitted on to a 1¼-inch rim and is pumped up to anything between 65 and 90 lbs per sq inch (the rating is marked on the tyre). HPs are almost invariably the best choice for any bike a little above the roadster, since they are relatively cheap, and it is easy to replace their inner tubes. They come in a staggering number of weights and patterns, and some of them approach 'tubular' racing tyres in performance. Very lightweight tyres are of course much more likely to crack or split under the heavy bumping and bashing of riding

around city streets, so for most purposes the middle range HPs are best. Keeping them well-pumped up is more important for easy riding than an especially narrow profile, but for those who want to get as close as possible to a racing performance, the narrow section HPs are becoming increasingly popular. Beware the varying sizes, though, and remember that if there is more than one rider in the household having the same sized equipment means that you can swap spares and tools in an emergency.

Tubular tyres, or 'tubs' are the universal choice of racers, hard-riders and the more elitist sort of commuter. Contrary to common belief, they do have an inner tube, but this is completely surrounded by a casing (of light material, in the best examples silk), and sewn up like a football. A thin tread of rubber is then smeared over this puff of air, and the entire tyre weighs-in at a handful of ounces. Weight does of course matter but the real advantages of tubs are these: because the tube is completely surrounded by the casing, it can be inflated to much higher pressures. If you over-inflate a wire-on HP tube, it will blow the tyre off the rim and the tube will burst. For a racer to whom comfort is secondary, indeed suspect, the harder the tyre the better.

The second advantage is in changing tyres if you have a puncture. A sprint rim is merely a shallow smooth-sided groove. The tub is easily rolled into the groove, and out of it, and is held in place by its own tension and a permanently tacky sort of glue. People who ride on tubs don't try to mend their tube when they get a puncture (in fact, many just take them back in batches to be repaired by professionals), they simply roll off the old casing and tube, roll on the new, a few strokes of the pump and they're ready to go. This sort of quick change is an obvious advantage in a race, but 30 seconds from puncture to pedalling away is a great comfort on a wet and wintry ride home from work as well. In case you have wondered, that untidy rubber parcel that almost all sporty bikes seem to have underneath the saddle is the spare tub. With no wire beading, they fold up easily.

The wheels and the frame are the two items where quality really counts. Always pay as much as you can afford for them because you will feel the difference, which is not always true of the highly priced baubles available. Most non-fanatics tend to judge a bike by its gearing, by the number of speeds. This is a hangover from childhood, as is the simple-minded literalness with which it is applied: three-speed good; five-speed better; ten-speed best. In fact there are two systems of gearing and each has its own advantages. The most common, certainly on runabout bikes, is the hub gear. The various cogs, pawls and springs necessary for variable gearing are all neatly packed away inside the hub, and the rider has only to worry about is the cable and the gear trigger. In England, luckily, there are no anxieties about quality with this gear since it's a dead certainty that the mechanism will have been made by Sturmey Archer, and, although they've had some problems with their new five-speed, two-lever version, they're as solid a concern as Raleigh's, with whom they are now associated. These gears are stunningly simple to use, and, as is often the way, idiot-proofing has been bought at the expense of some mechanical complexity. They can give a lifetime of service with no more attention than the occasional drop of oil, but if they do go wrong, seek expert help unless you're the sort of person who mends watches in your spare time.

Although the hub gear must be first choice for reliability and ease of maintenance, its ratios are an example of a compromise that doesn't quite come off. The gap is too wide for comfortable riding around town, yet it doesn't provide the extremes, of low gear particularly, that enable you to face the steep hill (every town, even in places like East Anglia, seems to have one) without a sinking heart.

Derailleur gears must be the first choice for comfortable riding because they provide so many choices. They're simple to understand, too, and it makes no difference if you're using 5 or 18 speeds. The freewheel block at the rear contains a cluster of different-sized cogs driven directly by the chain. The derailleur mechanism does exactly what its name implies: it moves the chain sideways until it 'derails' from one cog and jumps on to the next. It appears to be a coarse and ugly method, and the first few times you try it will sound like that as well, but in a very short time you'll have learnt the knack and the chain will jump from cog to cog with a sweetly satisfying clunk.

The usual freewheel block has 5 sprockets, though 6 or 7 can be obtained with the new thinner chains. By repeating the process at the pedalling end, and fitting a second chainwheel and a similar derailleur mechanism, you double the available number of gear ratios to 10 (or 12 or 14). Up to 3 chainwheels are fitted, though this makes changing quite complex and is really a specialised option for long-distance tourists. The advantage of this sort of gearing is that you have a big gear to enable those with the nerve to pedal down long hills at speeds in excess of 40 mph, and a very low gear which makes it possible to pedal — slowly to be sure — up any hill they've yet been able to build a road over. Having a wide choice of ratios in between makes it possible to at least come close to the cyclist's state of perfection: the ability to pedal smoothly and with unvarying rhythm over widely fluctuating terrain. The human engine can deliver over a surprisingly great range of speeds and effort, but it gives of its best over quite a narrow band. For comfort and efficiency, you should find that band and stay inside it.

The importance of brakes can hardly be exaggerated. There can be no compromises; you want the best stopping power you can get. Luckily this isn't going to cost you the arm and a leg that neglect of your braking system only too easily might. Provided you buy a decent respectable model and keep the brakes properly adjusted, then a tenner will bring you to a halt as well as a £100. The extra is paid for lightness, looks, and a greater, how shall we say, delicacy of operation. When you fling out the anchors, this is of marginal importance.

Brakes operated by solid metal rods are rarely found these days, except in children's bikes and certain models of deliberately nostalgic design. They will of course see you out, not to mention your children and your children's children, but I find you can never quite get the adjustment. Perhaps this is why people who've been used to riding old bikes find the brakes on a new model over-fierce. They've been used to squeezing as if the levers were a wrist exerciser.

Generally, brakes (like gear changers) are operated by cable. This means a wire is run through an outer casing of fixed length so that any movement at the lever end is exactly reproduced at the working end. Properly adjusted, less than ¾-inch movement at the brake lever should be enough to make the brakes begin to bite.

The mechanism is simply a caliper which forces two brake blocks on to the rim of the wheel and friction does the rest. There are two types. The centre pulls are the simplest, the most reliable and the cheapest. A scissor pivot is operated by the cable acting at the centre of a loop of wire. If you examine the mechanism you can see how simple it is and how, even if it has become a little lop-sided, the action of braking tends to pull everything back into line again.

The fashion now is for the side-pull arrangement, however, where the outer cable runs directly to the brake instead of to a hanger attached to the frame. In this the caliper is squeezed at the side instead of above, so that one arm is longer than the other. Obviously it would be much easier for this to go wrong, so that one block presses harder against the rim than the other. If you are spending a lot of money then there's little to choose between the types apart from looks, but if you are cost conscious you can run into trouble with a cheap side-pull.

Because bike braking seems so simple there are those who would like to change the principles entirely. One reason they haven't succeeded is the sheer efficiency of the old method. You are in effect using a disc brake with a 27-inch diameter disc, and the spokes make it a magnificent dissipator of heat. The problems come in the wet, for the rim is exposed to the elements, and comes within millimetres of the road at every revolution of the wheel. There is not much you can do by way of hardware to solve the problem — though alloy rims are much better than steel and you can buy special chrome-leather blocks that are more effective in the wet — so the answer lies in your riding. Try to keep the rims relatively clean by skimming them with the brakes every few minutes, and allow at least twice the stopping distance when you have to brake.

The most intimate parts of a bicycle are those where your body actually comes into contact with the machine. There are three: the saddle, the handlebars and the pedals. It must be admitted that one of the potential hazards of cycling is a sore crutch. The wrong clothing is often to blame, particularly jeans with thick raised seams, but that doesn't make the choice of saddle any less important. The wide 'mattress' saddle is usually fitted as a standard to ordinary roadster bikes, and because it seems to offer such broad-based support and is wire sprung, many people assume that it is the most comfortable and that the narrow 'racing' saddle is a concession to some complicated masochistic urge. The reverse is true. First, you don't need any such soft springing in the saddle, it only makes you bounce around insecurely out of rhythm with the bike. Second, the biggest problem is friction on the inside of the thighs as your legs pump up and down. The narrow saddle is designed that shape because that way you're less aware of it when you're riding — and the very best saddle is the one you forget about.

The best solution used to be a leather saddle — Brooks was the favourite make — which had to be treated with neatsfoot oil and saddle soap and ridden for 500 miles or so until you had beaten it into a compatible submission with your own shape. If you are going to do a lot of riding, or if you really are a peculiar shape, this is probably still the best road to follow, even if it's hard going at first.

Something seems to have happened to plastic saddles, however, which were once thought of as unyielding, awkward and sweaty. Perhaps the makers have just found out more about the shape of the human bottom. There's now a wide choice of comfortable plastic, or plastic and leather models which need no breaking in, are easy to look after and are often cheaper than leather. One interesting old idea that is making a comeback is

the so-called 'anatomical' saddle. This has a strange moulded shape, anatomical in looks in fact, but is designed particularly with women in mind to give the pelvic bones adequate support. It does seem a matter of personal proportion. Some people can climb on to any old mass-produced thing and find it comfortable for fifty miles a day; others, as sensitive in this area as the princess with the pea, try dozens before they find one that suits. The only test is your own comfort and satisfaction.

Handlebars are nothing more than a tube of either alloy or steel twisted into a shape. Either way they are cheap and the alloy will be lighter and corrosion free, but the choice is simply a matter of personal taste. That said, I think everyone should be riding on one of the versions of drop handlebar. It's nothing to do with racing snobbery, simply that the drops offer you a choice of some five riding

Another London-to-Brighton rider contemplates the Ditchling Beacon with mingled apprehension and determination. Each May town dwellers sortie out on the Sussex roads for the 56-mile back-roads jaunt to the coast.

positions, from crouched right over, which is rarely used except going into a wind when it makes a dramatic and welcome difference, to an almost upright, hands on the top, for stately progress looking to right or left. The only position these handlebars deny you is sitting full back with all the weight on the seat, and you should never ride like that anyway. It compresses the spine and transmits every jolt and jar from the road straight up the

29

back into your neck.

Assuming that you haven't bought something horrible from a market stall, most pedals will do their job (the criteria are that they should have a strong spindle that doesn't bend and proper ball bearing races). So the choice is again down to what feels best. Remembering that you will be pedalling with the ball of the foot and not with the pedal jammed into the arch of the foot against the heel, the most important thing is that your foot shouldn't slip off the pedal entirely. The best answer will be toe-clips (there's no record of anyone who has tried them reverting afterwards) but if you don't feel ready for them yet, steel 'rat-trap' pedals have a toothed edge to grip the shoe and can be fitted with clips later. I find that riding with rubber block pedals makes you permanently aware of your feet, like going for a walk across the field in your best shiny shoes.

This chapter gives no idea of exactly what it is that keeps cyclists awake for hours, while others fall asleep around them, talking about their machinery. Some of it is because you have to have ridden a lot of bicycles before the small differences that a change in head angle or tyre pressure can make become noticeable. And the other . . . Well, the East German Lothar Thoms took four seconds off the world record at the 1980 Olympics 1,000 m time trial. The distance is a sprint, so watchers assumed that this incredible margin was somehow connected with his incredible machine: an engineer's fantasy of no head tube or stem and hand-made individually streamlined spokes. Finally the Western press cornered the World Champion (he was that already) and asked what advantages the new design gave him. 'It doesn't give any advantage,' he said. 'The only thing it does is to make other competitors nervous.'

The spectrum of bicycles ranges from rather heavy, stolid machines of great mechanical reliability, through various compromises aimed at the commuter, the tourist, the back-streets racer, up to the hand-crafted thoroughbred that weighs in at less than the Christmas Turkey and is as nervous and temperamental as a racehorse — both to ride and to look after.

This is certainly a hierarchy of cost, but it is also a range of different purposes. Just as it would be foolish to try to race on a steel rattler, it would be a criminal waste of money to buy a racing bike if you only want something to take you shopping once a week. They all have their place.

As you go up the spectrum there are two gradual changes. First the frame tubing moves from seamed steel tubing, to cold-drawn steel tubing, then on to one of the specially developed bicycle steel alloys (Reynolds 531 and 735, Columbus) on to the pick of the bunch when each tube has a cross-section specially thickened at each end where most of the stress falls. This is known as double-butted and once you've moved into this class (you can still get a frame like this for about £120), there's nothing to choose between you and most of the riders in the Tour de France.

The other change is that more and more parts are made of lightweight alloy instead of steel. These are not only lighter, but they are often more precisely made. People who are willing to pay the extra for high quality brakes or gear changers would expect them to be alloy, so steel is usually found only in the very basic accessories. It's a long way from Raleigh's proud boast that they supplied the All-Steel bicycle, but the virtues they claimed for steel are still there. If you are trying to resurrect an old heap, or even trying a makeshift repair after an accident, steel is not only stronger, but more tolerant. The Duralumin, which is the most common alloy on bikes (95.5% aluminium, 3% copper, 1% manganese and ½% magnesium), has many advantages, but when bent or cracked, it usually has to be replaced.

It is the balance between these various qualities that makes a good bike, nothing to do with the configuration. One of the most common mistakes, for instance, on ready-to-ride bikes with derailleur gears, is to fit a close-ratio rear cluster which is no good for anything except racing. Just because it looks superficially like a sports bike, does not mean that it is best for city riding. Many commuters, for example, prefer plain North Road or butterfly handlebars because they imagine the extra height gives them a better view in traffic. Gears too are a matter of taste. However good wheels and a good frame will give anyone a more responsive ride, absorb the punishment of the road without wasting too much energy in flexing the bike itself, and provide the sort of luxury you don't have to be a connoisseur to appreciate.

Everybody dreams of being able to find their ideal machine for sale second-hand. Given adequate care, a bike will certainly outlast its owner so the only disadvantages of buying used is that the lustre will be lacking on the paint and you are likely to be that much nearer replacement time for cables and other bits and pieces.

The problem of buying second-hand is that all the responsibilities are your own. You examine the bike and make an offer for what you have seen. If it turns out later that the frame is bent — that's tough. With a new bike you would have a claim on the dealer. So, when buying second-hand, it is even more important to examine the machine carefully before purchase and, if you're unsure of your own competence, to take along a knowledgeable associate.

The best source of second-hand bikes is a friend, preferably one whose machine you have known and coveted for some time. This is a special case, but where possible try to buy from the previous owner instead of from an intermediary. Postcards in newsagents' windows, and small ads in the local paper are the most fruitful hunting grounds or, if you're looking for racing and specialised touring equipment, the classified section of the cycling papers.

At the top end of the market there is quite a

Yes, generations have used the handlebars to sling their shopping, but beware. The steering will be hard to handle and if there's a milk bottle in the bag it might pendulum into the spokes. Messy. There are better ways.

good trade in passed on machinery, but it is much harder to find a good middle-of-the-road bike. There are a few shops which sell them and, although their stock is usually tiny, these have often been reconditioned by a good mechanic and represent good value. Otherwise it is a question of patience and keeping a diligent eye open.

It is easier to find a real old rattler, and they can be picked up for a very few pounds, but the risks are correspondingly great. Weekly auctions are held in many towns, and every so often the police sell off the unclaimed stolen property from their stores. It's a matter of luck. Unless you are knowledgeable, your bargain may turn out to be so sick in its heart that it will never ride any better than it did when you gave it a trial squeak around the block. On the other hand, a few drops of oil and a wipe with a rag, new brake blocks and a few turns of the spanner, may give you a smooth-running steed that will go for ever.

For those who like to think big, corporate users of the bicycle often sell off their machines according to a schedule. These bikes are in widely varying condition and yet are usually priced at a job lot price per lorry-load. If you have fifty friends who are willing to pick over the spoils of a bid to the Post Office, you should all be able to get a decent machine for almost no money at all.

Chapter 3

Gears: Calculate Your Inches

HARDLY an enticing subject, gears. They bring to mind greasy hands and, worse, mathematics. Hard riders, whether tourists or racers, find gear ratios endlessly fascinating, and often seem to be riding round the country at great speed talking about nothing except 'overlap on the 16 tooth', but this only helps to make the subject even more impenetrable and irrelevant to the everyday traveller. As always, though, the easiest way to clear your mind of the matter is to bother to get it right. Once done, you can forget it and leave the tinkering after perfection to those whose compulsions run that way. This is true of a three-speed as much as a ten-speed, and, curiously, it's vital for a bike with only one speed — what some people might think of as a bike with no gears at all.

Since we're nearing the end of the second century of the Machine Age, everybody must be familiar with the principle of a gear. It is a device which alters the relationship between the power of a movement and the distance it travels. Assuming the machinery which works the trick to be completely efficient, which it never is, the relationship between force and distance is simple and direct: if you double one you halve the other. For cycling purposes gearing is the relationship between pedal revolutions and the distance the machine travels.

As to actual numbers it is a specialised world, but worth a brief visit, if only to get some idea of the reality behind the figures. A very common combination on stock bikes is a 52-tooth front with a 40-tooth front, and these chainwheels are allied to a rear cluster that begins with a small cog of 14 teeth. This gives a gear of just over 100 inches and it is far too high. You might need it coming down a steep hill at 35 mph if you wanted to accelerate the bike, otherwise it is there because that is what the racers have. I have overheard dealers trying to sell a middle-aged, mild-mannered tourist the necessity of a 100-inch-gear on the grounds that you will find yourself using it after a few months. This is nonsense. The only explanation is in some deep-seated machismo that says if Hinault can sprint to his finishes with a 53 — 13 (110 inches) then the rest of us should have one in reserve.

Gear ratios are complicated to talk about, since the variables spread outwards like ripples on a pond, but no run-of-the-mill rider needs a high of more than 90 inches (52 — 16, for instance) and the lower your low the better.

It's impossible to get a smooth run down through all 10 gears. The high of the small chainwheel will overlap with the lows of the large. All you can do is get hold of a gear table and work out the combinations as best you can by trial and error, remembering that you only really get 8 gears from a 10-speed set-up; biggest sprocket to biggest sprocket and smallest to smallest generally run the chain at too extreme an angle for mechanical comfort. Remember too that you must make sure the changer mechanism has a capacity to cope with the extremes of your sprocket size. Light-weight racing changers will be designed for close ratio gears only.

The simplest case is direct drive, where the pedals are directly attached to the axle of the driving wheel. One revolution of the pedals will mean one revolution of the wheel, so it follows that the larger the wheel the farther the bike travels for each turn of the pedals. This was how the old penny-farthings worked and partly accounts for their shape, as the fast riders went for bigger wheels and, therefore, a higher gear. The problem with this system is its inevitable and inflexible limiting factor. This is not the stress locked up in a spoked wheel 5 feet or more in diameter, but the inside-leg measurement of the rider. Look at any old picture of a penny-farthing rider and you can see that they are perched perilously within an inch of the rim so, if the wheel were any larger, they just wouldn't have long enough legs to turn the pedals.

This sort of drive is now only found on kiddies' tricycles and unicycles and will for ever remain outside the experience of most modern cyclists. It is therefore not surprising that it remains the basis, in Britain at least, from which all gearing is described. In other words a 76-inch gear is the same as a directly driven wheel of 76-inch diameter, had such a monster ever existed.

For riding around on the relatively flat roads of a town, you will probably find that a gear somewhere in the 70s will suit you best. You then need a couple quite close on either side to cope with the minor ups and downs of traffic conditions, railway bridges and the like. It is best to try and have this middle gear set for the large chainwheel and the middle sprocket of the rear cluster, as this will give a power gear in reserve and a similar but easier spread on the small chainwheel for headwinds, lazy days and rolling countryside. Then for the last, largest sprocket at the back, fit the biggest sprocket your derailleur can manage. When you hit a real hill, you can't have a gear too easy. Aim for the low thirties, as close to 30 inches as you can

Phillip Molloy's 'tribicle' was designed for weatherproof commuting, though aerodynamic faring and a reclining position are now finding supporters from the efficiency enthusiasts. Hand signals are still necessary, though, so you do get your arm wet.

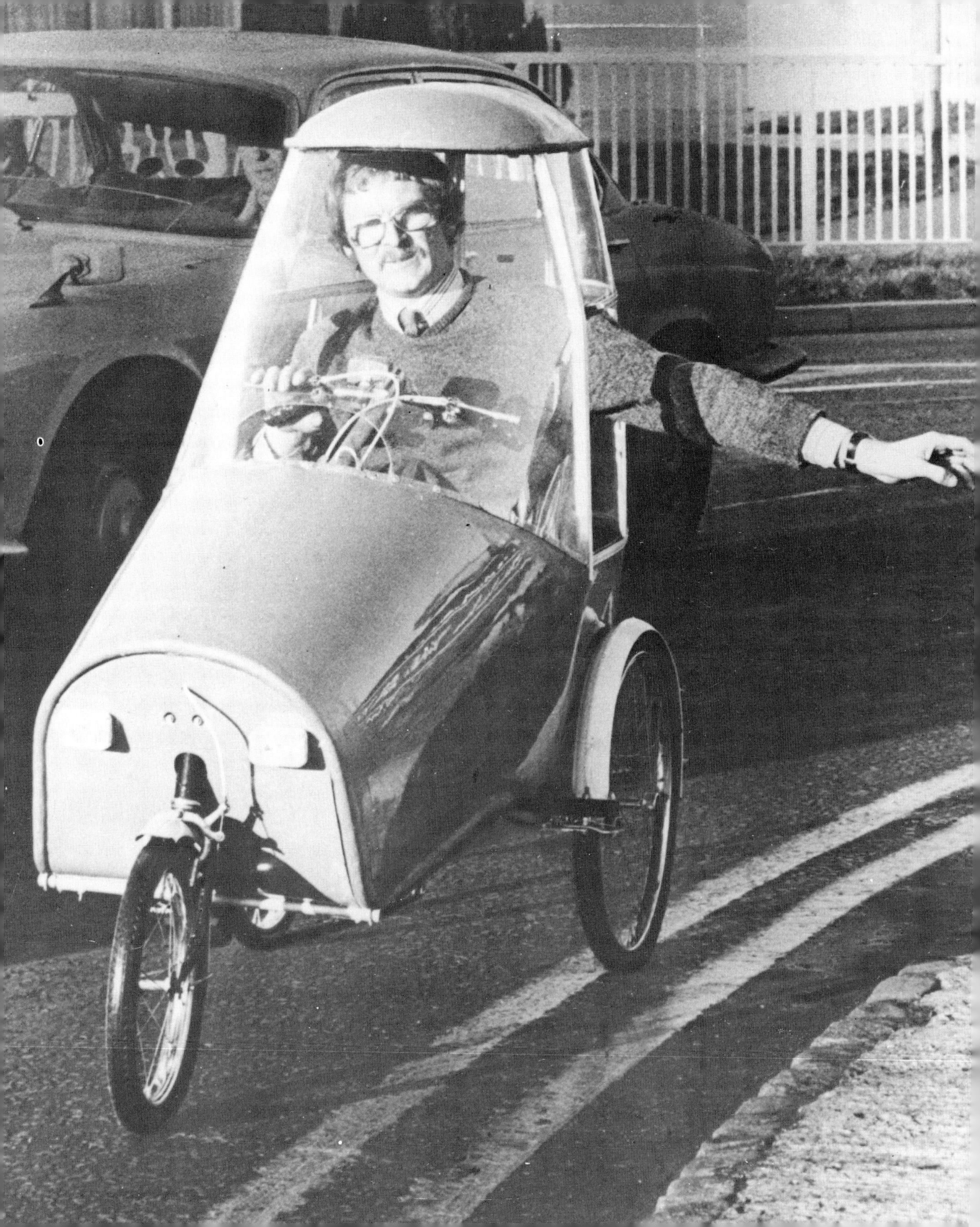

manage, and, as the tough testers of the bicycle guides are so fond of saying, you really will be able to climb the side of a house.

Nowadays a wheel is geared through the chain drive, and the formula for converting the effect into inchage is simple. Multiply the diameter of the wheel by the number of teeth on the front sprocket (chainwheel) and divide the answer by the number of teeth on the back sprocket. On the continent they simply assume a standard sized wheel and express their gears simply by the sprocket teeth, thus: 52 x 17. However, the English system does have the advantage that it's a single figure which requires no mental arithmetic to understand (52 x 17 for instance is the same gear as 46 x 15, that is 82.6 inches for a 27-inch wheel) and is applicable to any sort of gearing system and to any sort of bike, including those diddy little small-wheelers they call shoppers. On top of that, there's never any need to do even the one simple sum, since tables setting out all options are found in many handbooks and manuals.

Advantages Mechanical and Unmechanical

The secret of the importance of gears lies in the legs; they prefer going round at a certain speed. What that speed is depends on your fitness, practice and that private X-ingredient which determines your physical personality. There is no right answer, but a reasonable hench-mark might be 60 rpm for the ordinary cyclist-at-a-traffic-light, rising into the nineties for an experienced and keen rider, and disappearing into the hundreds for the fully-fledged racer. This speed of pedalling is called your cadence and can only be found by experience. As a further bar to getting it right first time, if you've just taken up cycling again, or have noticeably increased the amount you do, then your pedalling rate will almost certainly go up for the first six months or so.

There is of course no mechanical advantage to be got from gears. It still requires as much energy to move a certain weight a certain distance at whatever speed you pedal, so no contrivance of chains and cogs is going to turn you into a Hinault.

However, millions of miles of accumulated wisdom have proved that respect for the principles of cadence is the easiest and most efficient way to harvest the rewards of your efforts, especially over medium and long distances. In other words, suitable gearing means you will go further, faster.

Multiple Speeds

All this applies naturally and properly to a single-speed bike, and the subject of gearing is nowhere held as dear as in the hearts of that tiny band of pure-hearted obsessives who ride fixed wheel. Since they have only one gear, and their pedals, with feet attached, must continue turning with the wheel up hill and down dale, they have a particularly fine balance to strike, between creaking to a stop on a rise with a gear so high that their full weight is pushed back and up as the bike surrenders to gravity, and losing control as their legs fly off the whirlygig pedals on a steep descent. Most people prefer to confront the variety of the land by providing themselves with a choice of gears. The idea of multiple-gear systems is to allow you as nearly as possible to maintain your cadence whether climbing a hill in traffic, belting round a bypass or rolling down a lane. How near is nearly varies a lot from system to system. In practical terms you have a choice of two: either hub gears or derailleur.

Hub Gears

The classic three-speed is almost invariably in Britain made by Sturmey-Archer. The gearing mechanism is contained in the hub and is a superbly designed mechanic's nightmare of pawls and springs. For our purposes, this is a black-box operation: the unit does a certain job and, if it fails to do so (a rare event), then the unit is replaced without enquiring too deeply into what went wrong within. The hub works like this: the middle gear is direct drive, third gear is a 33 per cent increase in speed and first is a 29 per cent decrease. They also make a 5-speed hub with ratios like this: 1st −33.3%; 2nd −22.1%; 3rd 'normal'; 4th +26.6%;

5th +50%. What this actually means in 'inches' depends on the number of teeth on the chainwheel and the teeth on the (single) rear sprocket.

You can use these hubs to provide super high gears over 100 inches or low climbing gears in the thirties, but the gap between each setting is still quite large, making each change rather drastic. However, apart from regular oiling to keep out the rust, and the occasional check on the control cable tension, these gears require virtually no looking after. Once installed, they can be forgotten. Purists object to small amounts of energy that are wasted within the system itself, but against that this is undoubtedly the simplest system, from the rider's point of view, of providing multiple-gearing ratios.

To shift the whole set of ratios in one direction or another is merely a matter of changing the teeth on the rare sprocket, just as you would to find a better ratio on your single-speed bike. However, many cycle shops may prove strangely reluctant to do the job, as if you should put up with anything less than satisfactory because you're not riding a 'racer'. Be patient and polite, but persistent.

To change gear on a Sturmey Archer you stop pedalling. This might lose you vital momentum in the final metres of a Tour de France stage, but it does not mean you can change when stationary — picking an easier gear to start up, for instance, if you've been stopped at the lights.

The neat 'trigger' gear changers are best mounted on the front of the handlebars where you can reach them easily with your forefinger. They can however be nattily tucked away on almost any part of the front of the bike. You can also get twist-

Malcolm Clark, the builder of this bike, claims it was created to help him negotiate Northamptonshire during floods. For some reason, nobody else in the area ever copied the design.

grip changers, just like they have on motorbikes. These have been designed the wrong way round: looks first and function second. They are toys. If you want a motorbike and aren't old enough to drive one yet, why don't you get yourself a plastic construction kit?

Derailleurs

The derailleur gear mechanism is what they mean by '10 speed' though it is also common as a 5 speed, increasingly a 12 speed, and in every combination imaginable up to 24. These multiplex arrangements, though, are mechanically delicate and require a calculating skill from the rider. To get from one ratio to another often calls for considerable advance planning and a whole series of gear changes.

The 5-speed bike has one front chainwheel, and a 'block' of 5 sprockets at the back. There is one lever which moves the chain between the sprockets.

The 10-speed bike is the same as the 5-speed except it has 2 chainwheels and a second lever to move the chain between them. This doubles the number of ratios available since you get 5 on the large chainwheel and a different 5 on the small.

In practice, though, 2 of the ratios are unusable. Running the chain from the smallest chainwheel to the smallest sprocket, and from the largest to the largest involves too great an angle to be advisable for smooth running, or the health of teeth and chain. The largest rear sprocket is always closest to the frame and the largest front chainwheel is always furthest away from it. The chain is held on the selected place of the mechanism by the tension of the control cable which works against a spring. If unchecked the spring would always dump the chain on the smallest ring in each case. To change gear, the mechanism quite simply derails the chain from the sprocket it's running on and carries it over to another.

It's a brutally straightforward system, and it's a constant wonder that it in fact operates so reliably and smoothly, but it does require a certain subtlety of touch from the operator.

The technique of changing requires that the pedals be turning, otherwise the chain is not pulled on to the next set of teeth. However, you should ease up the pressure on the pedals just at the instant of derailing the chain to allow the whole operation to move smoothly.

Even when the chain is running on the correct sprockets, the changing mechanism can be improperly aligned, either front or back, which is bad for the derailleur as well as producing either a rubbing or a grating noise which you will come to hate as much as the sound of spade scraped across concrete.

It all sounds very difficult, but just as the accustomed hand can walk through a familiar house at night, cope with a dodgy doorknob and flush a highly eccentric lavatory, all on automatic pilot, so changing gears on your derailleur becomes second nature sooner than you'd think.

The advantage of the derailleur is that it offers the widest choice and greatest number of gear ratios, because, when not actually changing from sprocket to sprocket, the chain runs directly from driving wheel to driven cog, it has a very high transmission efficiency, wasting little energy in friction. But there is a certain aesthetic appeal, too. There it is, uncompromisingly out in the open, every cog and pivot open to the weather and the eye. The fact that it does require a certain modicum of skill to operate well takes nothing from its appeal to keen cyclists either. Anyway, it is almost universally used by sporting, long-distance and hard-riding cyclists and since they know only too well the cost in effort of inadequate machinery, it's safe to assume that no better method of gear changing has yet been devised.

Chapter 4

The Man with the Knowledge

THERE'S no reason why a well-chosen bike, treated decently, shouldn't figure in your will, so buying a bike is not something you do lightly, or often. Choosing the place where you buy the bike is the first decision you can get seriously wrong. The purchase price ought to include assembly by a competent mechanic, responsible advice and an after-sales service that will soothe anxieties as well as tighten nuts. That rules out discount houses, department stores, mail-order and streetmarkets (though not for second-hand, where different rules apply) and leaves you with your local bike dealer. Local is important

because, with an understandable sense of their own interests, bike shops show much more interest in keeping machines they sold themselves on the road, than in helping rectify problems which you brought on your own head by patronising their unscrupulous and untalented rivals. This not only means you can jump the queue for repairs (and that's a queue that can stretch into infinity, like a council-housing list) but it also sometimes brings the benefits of the shop's own bits and pieces tray which, stirred with an intelligent forefinger, can produce the spacing washer or bastard-sized screw that saves buying a whole new part.

At the top of the tree are the specialist lightweight dealers, who sell the machines and parts that the club racers use. Although friendly they manage to imply that, since you aren't intending to knock two minutes off your time for the fifty miles, why are you bothering them with your problems? Don't be fooled. More of their profits come from the likes of you than from the dedicated racers, most of whom know enough to sort out their own mechanical problems anyway.

Shops like this sell nothing but bikes and are easy enough to spot, but the most common sort of bike shop is also likely to be cluttered up with pedal cars, kiddie wheelbarrows and prams. The important thing is to distinguish between the bike shop which sells toys and the toy shop which sells bikes. Provided they can do at least basic repairs on the premises, you should be all right.

When you're buying a bike the two things you want from a shop are good assembly and good advice. The machines leave their factories in a half-completed state and it's the retailer who adjusts the chain, screws on the pedals and trims the brakes. You should always check the nuts and bolts yourself — it's your life you're about to entrust to the machine and it means more to you than to the most scrupulous mechanic — but knowing that someone competent did the job rather than a wrench-wielding savage does give confidence.

Picking the right bike is a complicated judgement which demands that you practise humility without getting overawed. Before you start you have to decide exactly what you want the bike for and how much you can pay. If your mind starts to fog over during negotiations these two facts give it something to hold on to.

The best bike for your purposes will always be a compromise — between weight and strength, between speed and comfort — and the dealer is the technician who should be able to translate what you want the bike for into the right combination of frame angles and gear ratios.

Just as important as choosing the right type is getting it in the right size. The responsible dealer should ask to see you straddling a bike, preferably several, and if he hasn't got one in the right size get

one ordered, don't buy a near-miss.

Most off-the-peg bikes come with gears that are a reasonable compromise between close-ratio and the sort of spread that will help you up steep hills. All the same, ask what the ratios are and don't be afraid to request changes — a bigger large sprocket at the back, for instance, if you want hill-climbing made easier (see chapter 3). Any decent shop should be willing to change the ratios at no extra cost, unless there is a difference between the cost of the component coming off and its replacement — and then you should only pay the difference. The same applies to saddles and mudguards. Few middle-range bikes have leather saddles as standard, but the dealer ought to allow the price of the regular saddle against that of a leather one. Sometimes the bike you've chosen will be equipped with some weird brand that is completely unsellable on its own. You can't expect to get any credit for that, but you can take it away with you and at least it's some sort of spare which, one day, might come in useful. The dealer also ought to be able to supply tools to fit all parts of your bike (spanners must fight their nuts exactly, otherwise the edges will gradually burr away into an ugly and ungrippable mess). The same goes for spares. If the shop can't supply replacements for any part of your bike, there is something funny about the bike or something wrong with the shop.

Most of the time all these cautions are completely unnecessary. The cycle trader usually knows what he's doing and has no desire to see some moneyed oaf tuck his slacks into his socks and wobble off down the street on six-hundred pounds sterling and nineteen pounds avoirdupois of finely tuned alloy. Apart from anything else, it's only storing up trouble for the future in the shape of a dissatisfied customer. On the other hand, most traders are, or were, keen cyclists themselves, and they equally don't want to see enthusiasm blunted by a machine that's too heavy and unresponsive to be any fun.

However — there's always an however — assuming that you've avoided the blandishments of the floor-walker in the pram department of the local store, there are two types around who may lead you astray. The most benign of these is the keen young racer learning the trade of mechanic down at his neighbourhood Aladdin's Cave. He looks about 17 and does the '25' in 56 minutes. Since he can't think of anything more desirable than Campag Super Record pedals at around £60 a throw, he imagines you can't either. Beware his enthusiasm. By the same token, and this applies not only to young Turks, assess your needs before deciding on such things as toe-clips and even crossbar versus a women's frame. Toe-clips do make cycling much easier and the traditional Diamond frame is by far the strongest and most resilient of normally encountered shapes, but if you know you will often be riding in skirts or clumpy shoes then compromise with discretion and settle for what suits your needs.

The other character to beware is a child of the present fashion for cycling and is to be found, as often as not, in shops with names like Hub Of The Town or Spokesman or Purple Pedals. Sometimes these shops are run by dedicated and brilliant mechanics, and sometimes by bodgers who took up the cycle business a week ago last Tuesday and believe that all mechanical problems can be solved with a hammer and a four-foot wrench. They always claim to be able to solve problems before they even know what they are, and will fix you up with a rear block your derailleur can't handle before you can say puncture repair kit.

Once you've found a dealer you can trust, you have somewhere to take those little problems that won't succumb to a day of swearing and grazed knuckles. It is humiliating to push your way through a crowd of customers with legs like anatomy drawings and explain, as I did, that you can't get your tyre back on, but the relief on finding that it was merely a matter of loosening the valve stem nut instead of tightening it was worth the shame.

One dealer, however, is unlikely to be able to supply everything you want by way of accessories. The same shop which is authoritative about mechanical matters, will often be conservative in such things as clothing, lighting, load carrying and special attachments. It's worth shopping around to find out who stocks the sort of shoes you like, who has the best socks and woolly hats, and where you can get such things as tennis racquet clips and American crash helmets. Often the best way is by mail order: you can find almost anything you need in the catalogues advertised in *Cycling* magazine, and sometimes it's the only way to buy, as with the tailor made plus-twos from Hebden Cord.

On the whole Britain is fortunate in its bike shops. When Alfred Morris left the cycle trade for the car business, he showed the way to the entrepreneurial go-getters who spent the early years trying to make a fortune from the bicycle, and what we have now is a network of mostly independent shops run by people as interested in bikes and biking as they are in making money. It is ironic, though, that in Raleigh we have the only serious industry left in which the biggest manufacturer is British.

A surprising number of these small and medium-sized businesses make their own bicycles, each modest high-street outlet topping a miniature production network of wheel builders, frame builders and enamellers. Such a custom-built bike is a remarkable bargain, costing little more than the best production bikes, and made exactly as you want it, down to the colour and transfers. You also get the benefit of all the experience of the builder when you're discussing how you want the bike to perform. By changing frame angles, fork rake, and chainstay (see chapter 2) the whole range of riding characteristics can be tailored to suit the customer. The danger is that the builder you pick, knowing so much more than you, will also assume that he knows much better. It's worth taking his advice at

OVERLEAF: *There are many ways of keeping dry, but this is not one of the commonly used ones. However, there are a lot of pigeons in towns these days.*

least half the time, but make sure he explains why he says what he does. There's usually a good reason, but once you know what it is, you can decide whether it's safe to ignore experience in favour of originality.

I don't know why he's looking so worried. The trains weren't running that day, so some people never got to work at all.

Chapter 5

Rhythm and Roll

RIDING a bike is as easy as falling off a log. Correct? Most of the population (well 78 per cent at the last count) can ride a bike and they learnt how on some golden day so far back in childhood that they can't remember exactly what it was like to lack faith in the balancing properties of a two-wheeler. Scientists, however, have still not worked out exactly how the trick is done. They talk of caster effect and gyroscopic forces, run equations of slip forces through the computers and one even tried to build an unrideable bicycle (he finally succeeded when he locked the front forks and tried to steer with the rear wheel), but in the end they decided it was a combination of a bit of this and so much of the other — as anybody who ever rode Auntie Elsa's Black Bess down to the pub could have told them.

Given forward motion a bicycle will stay upright and keep to a straight line without any help. The caster effect of the design of the front end means that the wheel is always trying to get back into line, provided the bike is straight. Lean the bike and the front wheel will turn. When you ride a bike you are making a series of minor adjustments to balance and steering to keep the bike straight and going where you want it. The secret of good riding is to

45

allow the controlling intelligence, if that's not too strong a phrase, and the machine to work together, not to muddle along despite each other.

All experts will tell you never to ride without hands, as this is foolhardy, unnecessarily flash, and likely to end in tears. They are of course right. I remember being overtaken downhill on one London to Brighton run by a youth with hands outstretched, sailing towards a bend as sweetly as a bird. It took but a small patch of mud and less than a blink to transform poetry in motion into a sorry heap of broken bike and bruised person. Every so often the bike will need you, and it's important to be there.

However, everyone should be able to ride without hands. It teaches you to use your body to balance and control the bike, and to understand without thinking about it what the natural movement of the machine feels like. It's also a good mechanical check since you won't be able to keep to a straight line with your hands off if the bearings between fork and frame are loose, the frame is warped or a wheel is buckled. It's a good idea to practise for a couple of hundred yards on every trip, just to make sure that your steed is fundamentally healthy and that you aren't sitting in the saddle like a sack of beans. Just make sure you practise on a quiet, flat bit of your route, with no cars about.

Happiness, as I've said, depends on feeling both comfortable and safe. Technique helps.

All the good intentions in the world about marking your presence in the right lane clearly, signalling decisively, and blending yourself with the flow of the traffic are so much saloon bar chat unless you can guarantee that the bike will go exactly where you intend. The cyclist most at risk is the one who can't keep to a straight line, which is why most of the casualties are children.

Americans believe in doing these things properly, and if the great guru of po-faced pedalling, Fred deLong, had his way, we would all form ourselves into self-help groups to practise such exercises as keeping to a dead straight line with one foot on the pedals, riding perfect figures of eight in convoy, and following commands suddenly signalled by an accomplice with different coloured flags.

I have my doubts. Apart from looking like a bunch of berks, and putting back the cause of cycling as a sophisticated transport a few years, military experience shows us that drill merely teaches the vice of unthinking obedience. Cycling, after all, is meant to be good for the soul as well as the economy. I'm a believer in on-the-bike training. As you are going about your business fix your eye on a leaf or cigarette butt a few yards ahead, make sure that your wheel hits it exactly. Keep practising. One day, when you are bombing down the alley between two buses and a TIR container lorry, and suddenly the road cracks into a moonscape just in front of you, it will save your life. The rest of the time it will make cycling easier and, as you learn to avoid glass and other rubbish, cut down your punctures.

Riding in a straight line is largely a matter of relaxing. Sit easily on the bike, holding the bars lightly, without clenching your hands, and the machine does most of the work. This is the basis of the technique for riding through potholes too. As any urban cyclist knows, the curbside half of the street is a necklace of holes and depressions strung on a ribbon of cracked tarmac and dusted with the glass dandruff of the motor car. In an ideal world you pick a relatively smooth course along this, but you should always be aware of what's happening on your offside shoulder. If a vehicle is coming past, you must resist the instinct to veer out, grit your teeth, pray for your wheels, and ride straight through the craters. The best position for survival

There are two sorts of flying bike; and this is one. Bicycle Motocross racers use specially built BMX machines to defy the laws of probability.

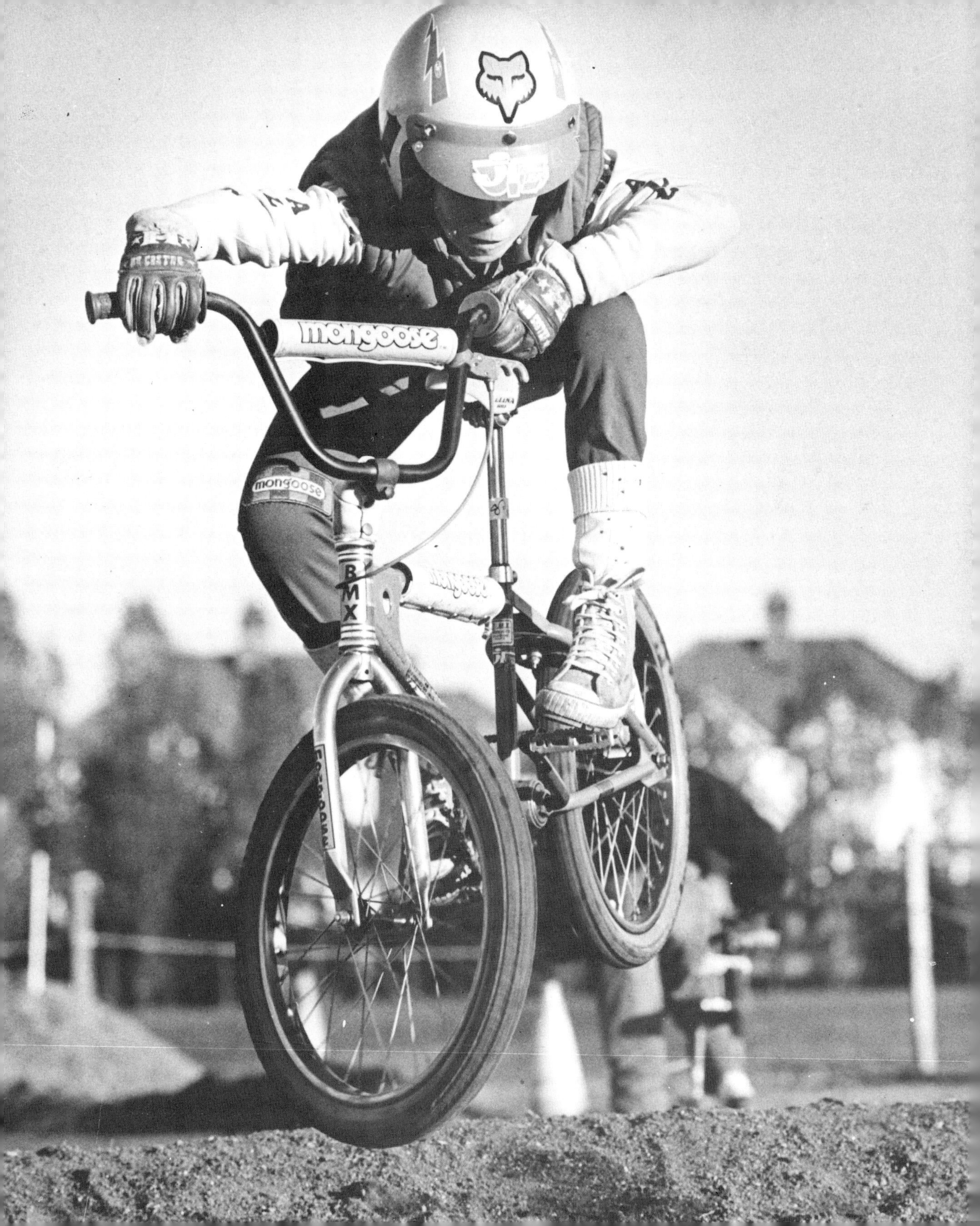
mongoose
mongoose
BMX

is to raise yourself off the saddle and spread the weight equally between bars and pedals. Hold the front wheel straight, but not too firmly, and allow the bike to flex beneath you. This not only saves your spine from jarring but lets the bike find its own way through the rapids. Legs and arms are shock absorbers, so keep them bent and relaxed, and the bike will ride out the rough ground like a cork in water. That's the theory, and it really does work.

One of the worst vices to have is rear glance drift. It's all too easy when you're peering over your shoulder trying to puzzle out the traffic behind, to drift gently out into the middle of the road. It's the natural consequence of worrying about drifting straight into the kerb. Concentrate until you can look back without moving off your line, but keep on looking behind you all the time. Since traffic is usually travelling faster than you are, what's going on behind you is more important than what's happening in front. Don't stare too long. Several eidetic glances will give you the information just as effectively, and more safely, than a prolonged squint. Turn your head to the right so that you catch anything coming up on your shoulder first. Trust the subliminal messages from the corners of your eyes. If you are crouched over it may be easier to duck your head down and look under your arm. Never jerk, if there isn't time for a deliberate look then something has gone wrong already.

Nobody needs to have safety sold to them, but the benefits of learning an efficient technique are less universally admired. I only ride a few miles to work, so why should I bother? Because you'll feel better, and get less tired. The human being on a bicycle is the most efficient self-propelled animal in the known world. It converts effort into motion more effectively than a cheetah, a salmon or a hawk. There may be figures to prove this but it's hard to take them seriously when you are labouring over a hump-back bridge. Yet with a little concentration on what you're doing it becomes credible. There is a moment of revelation when you're riding up a long hill and decide to pay attention to your ankling, when you suddenly look

up from your feet and find that, not only has the sense of toil disappeared, but you're actually accelerating.

The first step is to make sure the bike fits, and is properly adjusted for the rider. There are some splendid formulae available, such as 'a frame height of 12¾ inches less than the outside height of the head of the femur', but you'll do very well if you straddle the crosssbar with both feet flat on the ground and aim for a frame that gives about 1-inch clearance between the legs. On a step-through bike, straddle it and pretend that it has a crossbar.

Saddle height is again the subject of much high-flown argument, but there is a simple guideline which usually works. Sit squarely on the saddle and put the heel of your bare foot on the pedal. With the pedal at its furthest away from your hip, the knee should be straight without any tendency to shift your position. When pedalling with the ball of the foot, this height means that the knee never quite straightens out — which is as it should be. Many people find saddles this high awkward to begin with, so the other approach is to begin with the saddle set lower and gradually raise it over the weeks. A higher saddle means easier and more powerful pedalling, but don't raise it beyond the point where you can touch the ground with the toes of both feet when sitting down.

Handlebar height is a matter of taste. Adjustment is easy, so experiment. A good traditional starting place is with the flat of the bars level with the saddle. If you feel over stretched after a few weeks of riding, and if you find you always keep your arms straight, then the bars could be too far away. The seat can be moved forward in most cases, which has the advantage of bringing your hips more directly above the pedals, but if the problem continues it could be worth buying a new handlebar stem with a shorter extension.

The essence of riding comfortably is to find a smooth rhythm. The jerky, treadmill motion looks tiring, and it is. Most people ride in too high a gear for the speed they want, probably because of some distorted puritan feeling that work must not only be done, it must be felt to be done. A lower gear and quicker pedalling will get rid of a lot of the stamping, but there is an uneveness built into the very motion of pedalling. The natural pattern of force is from full power, when the crank is extended horizontally forward, to zero at the very top of the stroke: the so called dead point. The purpose of pedalling skill is to smooth out this power curve. The traditional method was ankling, flexing the foot so that it pushes forward and over at the top of the stroke, and back as well as down in the bottom half. It feels funny at first, and some literal-minded tourists of the old school have taken ankling so far that it is crippling, but it is worth persevering until a certain amount becomes second nature. A less precise variation is simply to concentrate on equal pressure throughout the stroke. This is easier if you have toe-clips, since your feet are firmly attached to the pedal. Imagine you have both feet dangling in a barrel of cream and you are trying to churn it into butter. Your speed will double for no apparent extra effort, and those hump-back bridges and long slow rises will flatten obediently in front of you.

A smooth rhythmic approach, and low gears, will get you up almost any hill, but out in the country roads have the habit of suddenly lurching upwards for a few yards at twice the prevailing gradient. Then is the time to rise gracefully out of the saddle and use your full weight to carry you over the hump.

In England this method of riding is rather frowned on by the purists, who call it honking. In France they call it dancing on the pedals and it is an accepted part of the repertoire. Even when you're up out of the saddle, though, a smooth, even rhythm should be aimed for. A lurching stamp is inefficient, and very tiring.

Honking is useful on long hills to give your muscles a break by bringing a different set into play, and it's exhilarating to climb up on to the pedals and fly over a small hump without changing down. On long hills, however, it is a bad mistake to stand up for a few yards and then find you haven't the momentum or the strength to sit down again and resume steady pedalling. You tire more quickly in this position so there may be no alternative but to get off and walk. And pedalling is an easier way of climbing a hill than walking, at least until your speed falls below balancing speed and the bike starts to veer from side to side.

Despite the example of sprint finishes in the Tour de France, it is bad style to have the bike dipping from side to side as you honk. In all modes of progression, aim for cycling perfection: the body perfectly still on the bike, the bike showing no movement from side to side, the feet revolving smoothly with the thighs parallel to the crossbar. It looks good, it feels good, and, by golly, it's efficient.

People, bikes and traffic lights.

Stick your arm out as far as possible and leave it there to allow even the slowest motorist to recognise it. The jersey on the right, though, dangling dangerously towards the spokes, is definitely not a good idea.

As a rider in town the man-made hazards of street layout and traffic will be the biggest obstructors of your progress, but every so often these may abate sufficiently for you to turn your attention to natural obstacles. The worst of these is wind and its ability to stop you in your tracks as if a giant hand was holding you back is a matter of direct experience. It is less obvious just how much relief a minimal amount of shelter or streamlining can bring.

If you are freewheeling down hill against the wind you can feel the bike pick up speed as soon as you crouch down over the handlebars, and even the shelter given by another cyclist can halve the effort required. Practise the technique of 'bit and bit' where two or more riders continually swap the lead, the follower hugging the wheel of the leader.

It can double your speed and cut fatigue. With a bit of practice it is like a train cutting through the air.

To be most effective, the leader should be changed every few minutes before the front runner's legs begin to ache. To avoid accidents the leader must ride smoothly, with a steady pace and no sudden stops or swerves. If you are going to change direction, shout out to those behind. The problem is that the front rider cuts the vision as well as the wind, so potholes and other obstacles are to be avoided or signalled for the others. Always leave room to swerve out of line when you are bit and bitting, and whatever the temptations never take the risk of slipstreaming behind a car or lorry. It's effective, but sometimes fatally so.

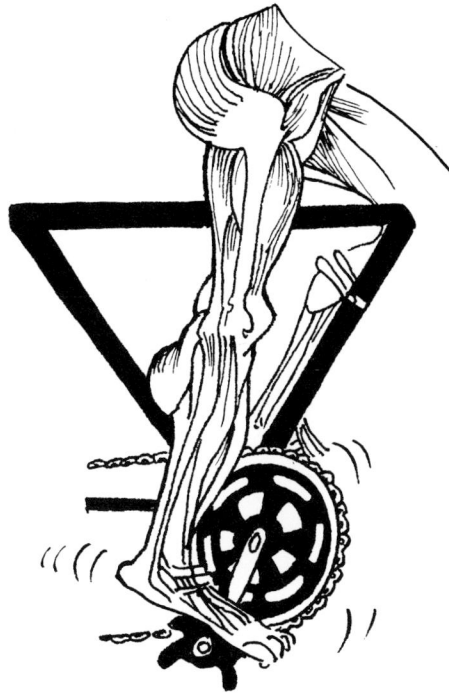

Chapter 6

The Soft Machine

CYCLING is exercise: the use of muscles, tendons, joints to make a physical mark on the environment. It is fairly mild exercise, to be sure (unless you are out there with the hard men turning the big 100-inch gears), somewhere between a gentle walk to the pub and dashing up two flights of stairs when you think you've left the bath running. All the same, any form of exercise has been held in such low esteem for so long that many people are still rather vague about the consequences. For instance, if you suddenly leap on a bike and pedal quickly for five miles to get to the pub before closing time, you may well find your breath coming in short, sharp gasps and your forehead bursting with moisture. Don't worry, you are not having a heart attack. What is more, this violent reaction will pretty well disappear after only a few weeks of regular cycling.

You will be fitter if you ride a bike regularly, but having said that let us leave the subject aside. There are too many people jogging round the parks, beating hell out of squash balls and cycling off on Sunday to picnics of low cholestrol sandwiches. There is no doubt that cycling rates quite a few points in the league of cardiovascular virtue, but we're not concerned here with how you

can cheat the actuaries and actually make a profit
on the insurance premiums. The benefits of using
your own strength to transport yourself around are
that you feel better, and that it's cheaper and more
reliable, not that it makes you live longer — though
it must be said that the evidence for that is very
strong. I'm assuming, therefore, that city cyclists
want to reach their destination in a reasonably
composed state, not in a muck sweat, breathless
and with a racing pulse.

Cycling is a very stress-free physical activity.
The basic pedalling action is smooth, and there is
none of the jarring and wrenching associated with
running, for instance, where each stride shakes up
the whole body. The mechanical injuries associated
with bike riding are all at the contact points: the
feet, the hands and the crutch. The constant
pressure at feet and hands sometimes leads to
numbness, pins and needles and pain rather like
pressing an old bruise. A complete cure can always
be achieved simply by rest, but you can also carry
on riding and, nine times out of ten, the problem
goes away. If it persists, then there are various
ways of relieving the pressure. Cycling shoes have
strong inflexible soles to spread the load over the
whole ball of the foot, but, if that doesn't work, and
you have made sure your foot is properly placed
with the toes pointing parallel to the frame, you
may have to consider changing the pedals
themselves. Some makes have a lip on the outside
which can stick up into the outside of the foot,
especially if your feet are broad.

Much the same principle applies with hands.
Cycling gloves have padded leather palms, with

*Maurice Carion's contrivance of flywheels,
pumps and springs is said to have many of the
characteristics of a Swiss watch. It's something
like a bike as well.*

extra padding at the base of the thumb, which make a considerable difference to your comfort. Another ploy is to fit the bars with a thick foam padding. Specially made closed-cell foam pieces are sold in bike shops, and they look neat, but even the most ham-fisted should be able to improvise something out of the odds and ends box.

Racing cyclists go through the most rigorous routines to ward off saddle sores and boils, one of the curses of their profession. The vulnerable areas are coated with lanolin before every race, and the chamois leather linings of their shorts dusted with talc. This could only too easily lead to bits of dirt trapped in the grease working into the skin, so on the long-stage races the whole area has to be scrupulously cleaned at the end of each day. If all this fails and something nasty does blow up, the time-honoured solutions are either to place a piece of raw steak between saddle and rider, or to cut a boil-sized hole in the saddle. Luckily this information is for titillation only, as boils are a rare complaint for average cyclists, and friction sores — more common — are a minor irritation. Both disappear of their own accord, and all the quicker if you take a few days off the bike. Inaction is cycling's most potent doctor.

The operating limits of the human engine are set by its ability to consume oxygen, and by the heat it generates. An averagely fit person riding a bicycle will be consuming oxygen at anything between three and six times the rate they do sitting in a chair. This can be kept up for hours in perfect comfort and breathing heavily is a pleasant enough sensation in itself. However, if you start to pant and gasp for air, it means your body is trying to use more oxygen than you can comfortably feed it. This is all very well for a special effort at the top of a hill, but, otherwise, slow down.

Overheating is more of a problem when you stop. Take away the cold rush of air that's been cooling it down and the body seems to wait two beats, just long enough to lock up the bike and walk into a shop or an office, then it pours out its calorific by-product in a long hot flush. There is nothing you can do except wait for the fit to pass. The heat has already been generated deep inside,

and splashing cold water on the face won't help at all. With a bit of practice you can learn to keep yourself the right side of the sweat threshold whenever you want to arrive somewhere in a cool, untroubled state.

Sadly for all those over-compensating motorists pedalling the rubber road to nowhere on the exercise machine in their bedrooms, cycling is a very poor method of slimming. Of course you do use up more energy, and burn up more calories, than if you were sitting in a car but the amount is relatively insignificant in weight-watching terms unless you ride for several hours a day — on a tour for instance. But then part of the appeal of touring on a bicycle is having the appetite and the excuse to consume enormous amounts of food. However, if you are riding briskly for any length of time you can suffer from the colourfully named bonk, or hunger knock, a sudden and quite dramatic weakness, which comes from not having the food available to power the muscles.

This can happen however much spare fat you are carrying around, since the body can't process the stored energy quickly enough. True bonk is rarely encountered by leisure cyclists, though it can provide a fascinating footnote to the plot of a big cycle race, but the faint stirrings are quite often felt, usually in the form of a compulsion towards something sweet.

If cycling is on the whole a benevolent activity, treating the body unusually kindly, falling off is quite another thing. The most likely injuries are bruises and scratches, but the risk of something worse, however remote, raises the vexed question of protective clothing.

Since the first instinct, if you take a flyer, is to ward off the ground with your hands, leather gloves are the protectors that bring most benefits, but what we are really talking about in cities is helmets. For a long time the protective headgear associated with cyclists was the familiar net of padded leather sausages, but since some research has been done into the matter it has been discovered that these provide almost no protection in the sort of accident an urban cyclist is likely to suffer. For a time various individuals experimented with adapted

They do things better abroad. Three different paths to take and clearly signposted for people and bikes.

climbing hats and skateboard helmets, but now designs intended for the cyclist are quite easily obtainable, although they are usually imported from America.

'Protect Your Thinker' says an advert for one of the helmets, and you can't quarrel with the sentiments. On the other hand, a helmet would be a serious limiter of the pleasure I get from cycling. It also seems to me that armouring yourself against your environment is quite the opposite of what cycling is all about. You can see how the awareness of being surrounded by metal and glass has dulled and blunted the reactions, however unconsciously, of motorists. They only react to their environment through the mechanical intermediary and somehow it takes the edge off your wits. Even in full body armour a cyclist's best defence against the risks of the city traffic are quickness of wit, and anything that takes the edge off . . . But these arguments were trotted out in vain by the (mostly

not at risk) diehards who wanted cricketers to face fast bowling with nothing more than pads, a box and a bat. Let's just say I like to feel the wind in my hair.

For a long time the invisible but nonetheless lethal dangers of a polluted atmosphere used to worry urban cyclists. Like almost everything sour in the cyclist's bowl of cherries, this comes from having to share our world with motor cars. As every urban dweller knows, the air we breathe is filled with choking fumes and the more insidious poisons of carbon monoxide and lead. The fear was that since cyclists breathe more heavily they must be more at risk. It's certainly true that on some mornings you can taste the nastiness of the air. However, a Dr Williams of London made tests on himself, riding ten miles through traffic to St Bartholomew's Hospital where they investigated the levels of carbon monoxide and lead in his system. They found nothing more than they would have expected in any Londoner. A romantic sense of the free spirit of biking, not to mention a sense of the ridiculous and a desire to breathe comfortably, would have prevented me from donning one of those smog masks that you see increasingly, but it is reassuring to learn that there is no particular reason why a cyclist should wear one. Indeed, a driver, without even the benefit of a stirred up metabolism to flush out his system, is probably more at risk from his own effluvia.

Grit or dust that gets in the eye can be dangerous as well as extremely uncomfortable. In bad cases the only safe course is to stop as soon as possible until the tears have done their job. For some strange reason this theoretically random problem doesn't affect everybody equally, and, if you find you're particularly susceptible, then goggles might help. However, they seriously interfere with peripheral vision and, since people who wear glasses seem to get a measure of protection from them, sunglasses could be a reasonable compromise.

I've studiously avoided cataloguing the general benefits of regular non-stressful exercise since they are hardly a special quality of cycling, but there has long been an underground rumour that sexually cyclists are at an advantage over the rest of the world. Recently there was an attempt to give scientific backing to the story with the theory that something called Cowper's Gland benefitted from the regular massaging it received from the saddle. I must confess I have never heard of Cowper's Gland in any other context, but since cyclists tend to be fitter and more sensitive both mentally and physically it has proved impossible to establish a control.

Chapter 7

Weather

THE weather, as every urban dweller turned urban cyclist soon discovers, is not a natural spectacle staged behind glass as a stimulus to conversation and wonder, it is environment to which you have to adapt. Our instincts now are all the other way around. Our indoor lives are designed to allow us to ignore the day to day variety in the outside world, and it is only with the greatest reluctance — and about a month too late — that the city dweller recognises the move from one season to the next.

Once you start cycling you are inevitably sensitised to the smallest shift in Nature's moods.

No good will come of trying to fight them with the same techniques as city builders. However much you swathe yourself in heavy clothing some rain will get through and you will feel unpleasantly stifled and damp. The spaceman strategy of carrying your own 'ideal' environment around with you won't do. The only sensible thing is to fit yourself to what's going on in the weather, accept it, and make the best of it. After all, the weather has been much the same since we hominids crawled out of the primate thicket, and we have adapted to it. Our skin, for instance, unlike any fabric or material, is perfectly and comfortably waterproof.

If you're going to practise fitting in with the environment you have to adapt your behaviour. The most obvious, and probably most important thing you can change is what you wear, and that is dealt with in the next chapter. There are other ways, though, in which you acknowledge a change in the weather conditions, and these mostly come under the heading of attitude.

The Wet

The first thing most idly curious non-cyclists ask a two-wheeled commuter is: 'what do you do when it rains?' The answer is, usually, carry-on cycling, but this can be carried to extremes of obstinacy that are not only wildly uncomfortable but dangerous. Just as the peoples of the arctic are said to have more than thirty different words for snow, each one with a slightly different meaning, so the cyclist learns that rain comes in many manners and degrees, and at some point on this spectrum there is a cut off point when it's not worth cycling any more than thirty words for snow, each one with a slightly different meaning, so the cyclist learns that rain comes in many manners and degrees, and at some point on this spectrum there is a cut off point when it's not worth cycling any more. This point, which is different for everyone, and for one person varies from day to day, could be said to be when it's less unpleasant to travel by few spots of rain are enough to drive them back into the travelling boxes of rail and road.

It is undoubtedly more dangerous to ride in the rain than in the dry, and as always most of the greater hazard comes from other users of the road. When it is wet the fat tyres of a car can all too easily find themselves rolling over a thin film of water instead of sticking to the asphalt. The deep and intricate treads cut into car tyres are designed to channel away the water, and they're not found on bike tyres because, with their narrow cross section, this is not nearly such a problem. On the whole you can expect your grip on the road to be nearly as good as normal when it's raining, but it won't be true of those around you. So the first rule of riding in the rain is to make even greater allowances for erratic behaviour from motor vehicles. If there's a tempting gap, just you and a smidgeon wide, between that six-wheeled truck and the kerb, then resist the temptation to slip through it when the road is wet. Especially on a bend and most especially on an outside bend, because that's the way the wagon's going to roll if it does start to slide.

There are three banana skins to watch out for too. They are mud, leaves and metal roadware. Mud and leaves are perhaps obvious, and should be approached with caution at all times, but the catseye or manhole cover which presents no problem in the dry can become instantly lethal when it's slicked with a thin layer of that iridescent oil and water mixture the city streets sweat in bad weather. As always, if you spot a hazard which you can't avoid, keep the wheels in line, the bike upright, the weight on your hands, your mind on your balance and your fingers crossed.

Brakes

If sticking to the road is no great problem, stopping in the wet is a quite different matter. Car brakes may fade but bicycle brakes just disappear. Almost all bicycles use the rim brake which, for all its simplicity, is a remarkably efficient system. However every revolution of the wheel brings every part of the rim down to within an inch of the road, and this means that in the rain your braking surface is thoroughly coated with a fine spray of oil and water. When you apply the brakes in these circumstances, nothing happens except that your

Provided your car is as wide as the bike is long, this sort of removable carrier (TOP) is a better solution for a lift out into the country than stuffing it into the boot.

heart drops through to the saddle. It's perfectly all right to panic as you glide with undiminished momentum towards the back of a coal truck, but remember to keep the brakes hard on. They will work, and quite suddenly, once the pads have dried the rims.

In order to avoid such horrifying moments, allow at least twice the stopping distance and apply the brakes fiercely at the beginning just as you shouldn't when the rims are dry. It's also a good idea to squeeze the brakes lightly every five minutes or so to clear any mud or muck from the rims, and to do this particularly when approaching a junction or sharp corner where the brakes are likely to be needed. It sounds as if you have to do a lot of thinking but it soon becomes a habit to keep trying the brakes in the rain, and it's surprising how efficiently the unconscious adjusts to what seems the natural braking distance to allow for conditions.

Mechanically, there are no efficient methods to counter the effect of rain on your brakes. The coaster brake which is operated by back pedalling is, it's true, almost unaffected by the weather, but it is not really satisfactory in other respects. Some brake pads, the chrome leather variety, claim to be, and are, much more efficient in the wet, though they are rather spongy in effect the rest of the time and are also several times more expensive. If you are likely to ride regularly in the rain then this is a good enough reason in itself for fitting wheels with alloy rims. Steel makes the worst possible braking surface. It is best though to place little trust in mechanical solutions to the problem of rain — instead keep your machine clean and improve your riding habits.

Cleanliness may be a matter of pride, but it is also good sense, sound economics and safer. The muck your bike picks up from a wet road is not just unsightly, it's also a sinister compound of grits, oil, salt and any other nasty effluvia scattered into the environment by the petrochemical industry. On the frame itself it encourages corrosion, on brakes and gear changers it clogs the operation and on chain and sprockets it increases wear by turning your lubrication into a packed layer of abrasive.

Instead of smoothly engaging metal surfaces you have the effect of two rasps working in opposite directions. To slap more oil on top of such a mechanical nightmare merely worsens the case. The only cure is to clean chain and sprockets with petrol or spirit until you are back to bare surfaces, and then lubricate again.

One of the most sinister and nerve-wearing effects of rain is that it forms puddles. It is not so much that they splash up and soak your toes, it is that you cannot see beneath their surface. The car driver swishes blithely on, confident that these flat surfaces of water conceal nothing that threatens, the cyclist cannot be so cavalier. A ten-foot wide puddle may hide nothing more than the merest hollow in the road, a two-foot puddle may be sitting over a foot-deep pothole. If you possibly can always ride round the outskirts of a puddle. If it can't be avoided because of the traffic, then ride through it very slowly indeed.

This makes it sound as if riding in the rain is some sort of ordeal, a thing to be endured rather than enjoyed. That's not true at all. It will become an ordeal, though, if you treat it in the same way as riding in the dry. Take the matter of speed. It is much harder to read the road ahead if it's shining wet and covered with puddles of unfathomable depths. This is even worse at night in the city, when the low level (compared with the sun that is) of the street lights make every sheet of water glitter like ice and every small bump cast an overstretched shadow. You can almost hear the zither of The Third Man in the humming of the wheels. The answer is: slow down until you feel comfortable. There is an instinct inside you which knows the answer, so learn to trust it. This applies in all weathers and perhaps most especially when freewheeling down steep hills. There usually comes a time when you are seized of a sudden suspicion that control of what is happening is just about to pass from you to the whim of the gods. This is the moment to put on the brakes. To modify the old black joke, panic is Nature's way of telling you to slow up.

Wetness comes naturally with the rain, but when you're riding a bicycle it's not the stuff that falls from the sky you should worry about. Except in the very worst downpour, it's fairly easy to protect yourself against that. No, the really penetrating moisture comes back at you off the road. The first agent of its resurrection is your own tyres, and this can be easily avoided just by fitting full mudguards. It may look sporty to do without, and there is a certain truth in the fact that a guard is like a small sail, adding appreciably to your wind resistance, but without them you will get sprayed all over in general and in particular have a broad muddy stripe painted up your front and down your back. Mudguards are one of the rare cases in cycling where a compromise is no answer at all. Either fit full guards with a proper mudflap on the bottom, or brave the spray, but don't waste energy or money on the so-called racing mudguard, a five- or six-inch strip which serves no purpose except to feed the fantasies of children.

What you cannot avoid is the water thrown up by other vehicles. The big splash that comes when a car runs through a small lake right next to you is annoying enough, for pedestrians as well, and the way most cars are driven as if these puddles weren't even there, is a telling indication of how being shut in a motor vehicle cuts you off from what is really going on in the world around. On a bike this particular nuisance can usually be avoided by keeping your distance from other traffic and making pointed detours round open expanses of water to force others away from them.

All cars and lorries throw up a more insidious spray from their tyres which cannot be avoided. It's a fine, almost invisible mist, well fixed with grease from the road, which has the wetting capacity of a swim in the Channel. It hangs in the air like a cloud behind all motor vehicles. With a car you can avoid the thickest by keeping at least fifteen feet away but the spray thrown by a lorry seems to hang for hundreds of feet behind, so there's no avoiding it. If there is relatively little traffic, though, then beware being overtaken in the rain. The sudden shock of being hit by this shower, just when your instinct tells you the danger has past, can be most unbalancing.

Spectacles and Hats

Although the next chapter is about clothing, here is a little interlude on the problems of people who wear spectacles. Although the best way to deal with rain generally is to remind yourself that a little water never hurt anyone yet and, taking a tip from Gene Kelly, give yourself over to the enjoyment of the special sights and sounds and smells of rainswept streets, it must be said that people who wear glasses do have special problems. Rain on your lenses makes it impossible to see. It is not practical to stop every so often to wipe them clear, and nobody has yet, so far as I know, come up with an acceptable method of mechanical wiping. The only answer is to keep the rain off the lenses in the first place, and the only way of doing this is with some sort of brimmed hat.

I have experimented endlessly with hats and caps and talked to others with the same problem. In the end everybody has to go through the same process, but here are a few hard-won thoughts which may shorten the period of experiment.

First, of course, the hat must stay on, so although it is possible to improvise arrangements with chin straps and the like, nearly all of the standard hats and bonnets that pedestrians favour are ruled out. Most people are going to settle for some sort of brimmed cap. Contrary to expectations a particularly long peak, such as motor mechanics wear in the pits, is not especially effective. It just gives the wind more to catch hold of. The principle seems to be to go for a brim that comes sharply down over the eyes, in the manner of those ridiculously shiny things you see on Guardsmen. Then you get down on the bars and squint upwards just under the brim. It sounds an unlikely recipe for success but you will be able to see. The light cotton casquettes (or racing caps) the sporting cyclists wear are quite good for this. In fact, they're highly useful altogether: they also keep the sun out of your eyes or, turned back to front, off your neck. They cost almost nothing, and, if you have the right sort of standing, you can even rent out space on your cap to advertisers. When the weather gets colder, most sporting cycle shops will be able to sell you a thing called a training cap. This is much like a knitted ski cap which folds down over the ears, except that it has a little peak. A more stylish alternative might be a deerstalker.

These devices may keep the rain off, but they are little help against spray from the road. The only answer I've found is to duck your head and brake whenever you detect some monster sluicing past dragging its cloud of spray. It sounds defeatist but then sometimes God is on the side of the big battalions.

Incidentally, if you do find that all these peaks, combined with a perfectly natural desire to do evens down the Old Kent Road, mean that your glasses get steamed up, try rinsing them with washing up liquid and then cleaning them.

Wind

If the cyclist has an enemy in Nature it's the little round-cheeked cherub with the pursed lips you find on the margins of old maps. Non cyclists may think that rain and hills are what we fear but in fact the only really hostile force is the wind. As explained elsewhere, more than 90 per cent of the force required to travel at 25 mph is used in overcoming air resistance, and to increase one's speed to 30 mph would require as much force again, at which point all other obstacles to progress have become effectively negligible. The most disheartening experience on a bike is to climb a steep hill in the honest expectation of a well-earned swoop down the other side, only to find when you put your wheel to the descent that the bike won't actually move without hard pedalling because of the wind. Doing one's best with this is a matter of riding technique and belongs in another chapter, the point is that wind is the only element of nature that can truly make you miserable.

Snow

Snow is almost always exhilarating and rather beautiful, so, although its effects on a city cyclist are much the same as rain, there's an added pleasure in riding through a snowfall, especially as

a bicycle is the only means of wheeled transport that lets you enjoy the peculiar quietness of snow, with each sound sharp and distinct. A blizzard out in the country is another matter. You are likely to get chilled, it's hard to see the road, the bicycle becomes difficult to handle and solid lumps pack under the mudguards. If you have got good clothing and keep your head, and don't try anything absolutely stupid like crossing the Pennines at midnight, the discomfort remains but at least there is no danger — from the weather at least — and the satisfactions of making it through such conditions can be immense. On the other hand, if you try to travel through a snowstorm on lonely roads in inadequate clothing, there is a very real risk of exposure.

Most people prefer to stay indoors when the snow is falling, but afterwards it can lie on the ground for weeks. New-fallen snow is little problem on a bike, though it can feel laboriously like wading through water. After a time, however, it becomes packed and rutted. Such a surface is obviously treacherous to all vehicles, but it can become almost impossible for a bicycle. Unlike a car, you haven't the weight to break through the walls of a refrozen tyre track, and it's all too easy to find yourself gliding merrily round a corner you never intended to take merely because you're locked into the path a lorry took that morning. In cities, however, these conditions rarely last more than a few hours, since the other traffic, in a rare benevolent role as a King Wenceslas, will have carved a path you can follow. The rule here is always to centre yourself exactly in the tyre tracks, ignoring the rest of the road, however innocently

The actor's touch. Sam Wanamaker, on his way to the Globe Theatre, demonstrates the Shakespearean hand signal.

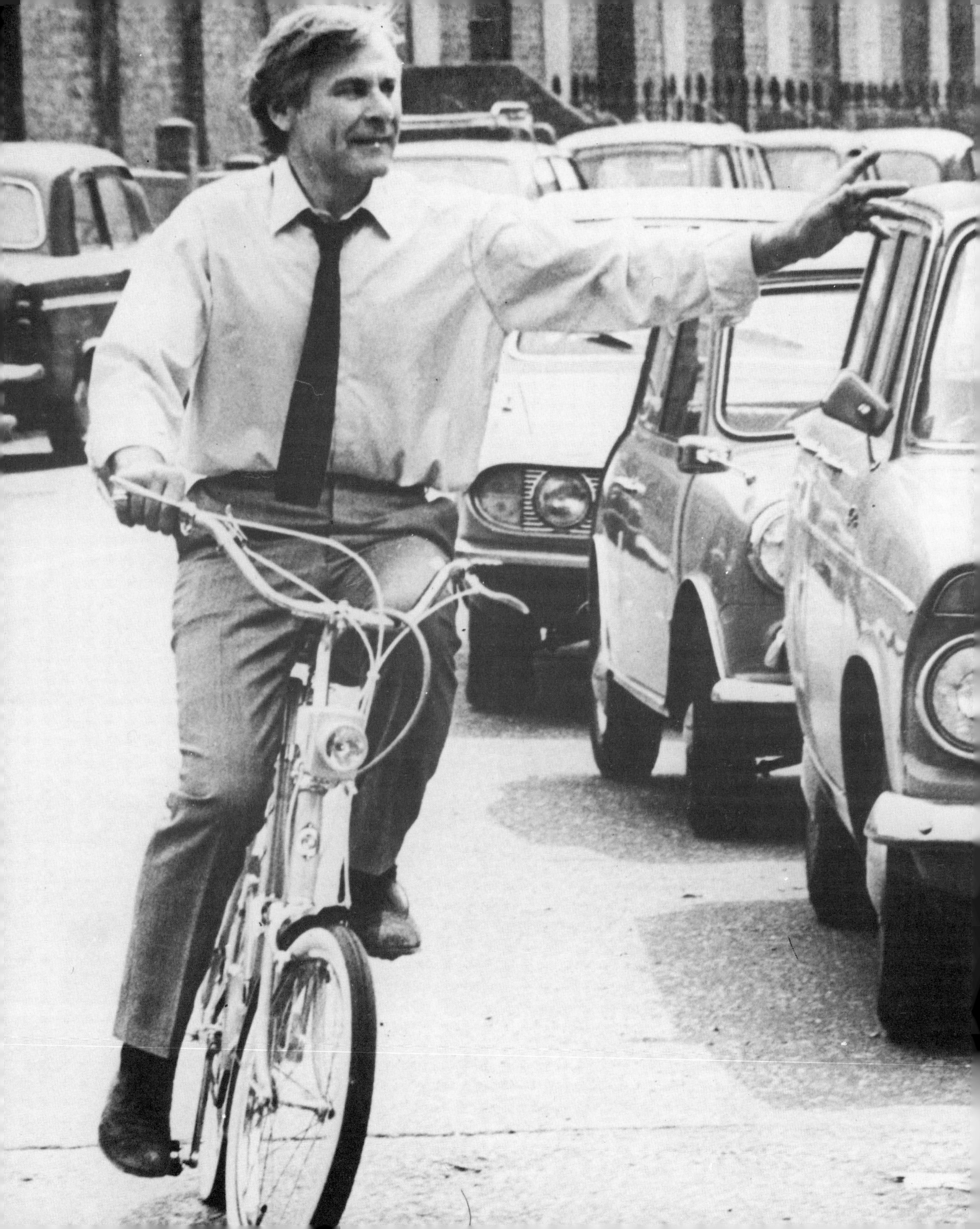

smooth it looks, and keep all your senses alert for that free fall sensation in the stomach which means you've hit an icy patch.

The Seasons

All these precautionary comments must sound intimidating if you're reading them in a comfortable armchair in a home to which you've been carried by train, but that's not a fair impression. One of the great pleasures of cycling is that it does get you out into the open regularly, so you're forced to appreciate not only that the seasons change, but that they all have their own pleasures and beauties, none of which will be enjoyed unless you accommodate yourself to the conditions. It's impossible to choose between cycling to work on a chill March morning, spotting a faint wash of green on the bare trees and announcing to those you work with that Spring has arrived — they won't have the faintest idea what you're talking about — and cycling home late of an August evening through air so warm it's like a bath.

The Sun

The sun, so we read in reports of the Tour de France, can be a pitiless orb, sapping the strength and draining the will. Certainly it played its part in the death on the Mont Ventoux of Tommy Simpson in 1967. It's rarely like that for the ordinary rider in Britain. The biggest problem comes from glare. On a bright summer's day it's an obvious precaution to take sunglasses, or a peaked cotton cap, but in fact for a city rider dazzle is at its worst at the ends of the year.

If you work to the East of your home then riding in the morning can often involve staring down a long street straight into the newly risen sun, and by the time you're travelling home, the damned thing is setting straight into your eyes again. This seriously affects how much of the traffic you see. Never mind that the sun is weak and the air is cold, dark glasses are the only effective solution. In a city you are likely to be shaded from the glare by buildings for most of your journey. This makes the sudden brightness shining through the gaps at a junction even more alarming. Watch out for it.

Chapter 8

Clothing

IF there is one secret to enjoying using a bicycle for your transport it is to get what you wear right. The wrong clothes can easily produce extreme discomfort: chaffing between the legs, tightness under the arms or across the chest, irritating cold spots in the small of the back. These problems can be easily diagnosed, however, and are simple to put right. Less obvious dissatisfactions can also be traced to clothing, and these are much easier to ignore. You know you're not enjoying yourself but you never bother to work out why.

If you travel to work in an office, for instance, you may find yourself feeling intensely irritated by little frustrations, shouting with unnecessary bitterness at other road users (righteous anger at car drivers is all very well, but you shouldn't let it eat you up); groaning miserably instead of ruefully every time the weather is less than a perfect dry morning. Sometimes the cure is simple. These are just symptoms of anxiety about your clothes brought on because you're trying to travel in the same clothes you'll be working in. I remember once getting so soaked that I had to hang around waiting for the shops to open so I could buy a new pair of trousers to spend the day in. It is extremely antisocial, not to mention undignified, to hold a conversation while you're gently steaming. Nothing can spoil a party quite so easily as the discovery that you've just smeared chain grease all over your new beige trousers. The only completely satisfactory answer is to change.

The main purpose of cycling clothes is temperature control. They should also be comfortable, of course, but that is largely a matter of long enough, loose enough and seams. Long enough to cover all they should when you're stretched forward, loose enough not to restrict you when you're moving, and built in such a way that no heavy seams are trapped between you and the saddle. Temperature in a bike rider is a matter of conflicting extremes.

Most journeys contain a variation of the switch-back pattern which professional riders blame for the incidence of bronchitis in their trade. This comes from the fact that one minute you're toiling up a hill, working fairly hard and travelling fairly slowly, so that your body is getting hotter and hotter and you feel like stripping down to a T-shirt, then the next you're swooping down the other side, hardly working at all and being rapidly refrigerated by a 35 mph jetstream round your ears. There will never be a satisfactory answer for those who race over the Alps for a living, but more modest activities can be accommodated.

The principle is simply to dress yourself in layers. Several thin tops are not only better insulation than one thick one, but they allow you to make fine adjustments. With four layers ranging from T-shirt or vest to a wind-cutting jacket, it should be possible to cope comfortably with almost anything that British weather can throw at you.

There are two techniques which can be adapted for fine control of your temperature while on the move. They are The Zip and The Hat. If you make sure that the top garment you're wearing has a front zip, then you can infinitely adjust the amount of cooling breeze that gets through to the layer beneath. Up to the neck and it's a complete extra skin, fully open and it might as well be in your saddlebag, with as many stages as you want in between.

Less flexible but even more dramatic is The Hat.

About 30 per cent of our heat loss is through the head, but this can be cut by at least half by an effective woolly hat or training cap. The trick is to arrange the layers so that you are comfortable with the hat on and you are pedalling easily. Then, if competitiveness or a steep hill pushes you into greater exertion and you start to heat up, simply pull off the hat. It's like taking the lid off a saucepan of boiling water. I used to use this trick to cope with delayed sweating. You are likely to be most hot and bothered in the few minutes after you've just got off your bike. The body is still flushed from exercise but the cooling fan of your rush through the air has been abruptly switched off. This can come as a surprise when you're not used to it.

When I worked on the twenty-something floor of a high-rise block I used to swoop in through the curved drive, padlock my bike to the railings, nod graciously to the commissionaires and step into the lift. Just as everyone was shuffling closer together to squeeze in the last half-dozen, carefully avoiding each other's eyes or aggressively intimate arm movements, drops of water would suddenly blossom along my forehead and down my back as if on the surface of a brutally squeezed sponge. There was nothing to be done except stare miserably at the floor. Neither wiping nor rinsing in iced water could do anything to shorten the fit. However, in winter you can pull off your hat for the last mile or so and fight off the deep heat of exercise with the fundamental coolth of a chilled head. It works. In summer there is not much you can do except wear as little as possible and take it easy for the last half of the journey.

This matter of untimely sweating leads on to another embarrassment. Like the idle rulers of the Eighteenth Century we like to show our civilisation by shunning all signs of physical exercise. It's bad enough when your morning gets somewhat compressed and flustered but when you find yourself trying to hold the first serious conversation of the day with perspiration dripping from your face to the floor . . . it happens to all cyclists sooner or later, but many people draw the line at arriving at work in shorts and T-shirt. However, things are getting better now that squash and jogging have become the hallmarks of the upwardly mobile and the knobbly knee is becoming accepted in polite society. More and more workplaces are now providing showers, and they're all obliged to provide a lavatory which will do perfectly well as a changing room. But if you're determined to ride a bike to work, or to see friends in the same clothes you would wear for driving a car, and you're happy to live with a wilting shirt and a chaffing waistband, then, fair enough. For the rest, here is brief guide to some of the more sensible options, starting from the bottom.

Feet

The requirements of a shoe for cycling are that it should be cut away from the ankle, to avoid rubbing, and that the sole should be flat and stiff. If you do use toeclips, and apart from making pedalling easier they also allow a greater range of shoes to be worn without your feet slipping off the pedals, then the uppers should be smooth and fairly narrow so they can be easily thrust into the clip and, more importantly, easily pulled out again. High heels may look a little incongruous, but they are neither here nor there. A cycling shoe has no heel because that part of the foot is not needed, equally a three-inch stiletto may look funny, but it doesn't get in the way. Gym shoes are traditionally frowned upon, because the sole is soft, but in fact it's also thick enough to stop the pedal cutting in to your foot and convenient to wear on or off the bike. And cheap too. Training shoes can be even better, though beware the hard sawstooth tread on some of them, which can glue your foot to the pedal at inconvenient moments like an emergency stop. Some of the more exuberant designs also have dangerously intricate mouldings and stitchings on the upper which can snag on the clip if you don't take care.

Cycling shoes proper range from extravagantly supple light pumps in perforated Italian leather with no heel — which cost a fortune — to touring shoes which are similar to the traditional English walking shoe. If you are sure you have another pair to change into at your destination, then a middle-

rank cycling shoe, with a very thin heel, is pleasant to ride in around town. Almost all the racing shoes are designed to be worn with cleats, a shaped block set into the sole which actually locks your foot to the pedal, but this is certainly unnecessary in town, and probably makes you feel insecure as well. A good compromise is the training shoe made by Bata which has been designed for bikes and incorporates some of the more useful features of a cycling shoe without actually crippling you when you walk.

Most cycling shoes are black, and the only discernible reason is that it looks good. These muscle-bound heroes are not unaware of what a stirring sight they make humming round the bend in full fig, and they long ago decided that the elements which best set off the lurid patterns of their racing jerseys and the brightwork of their enamels were black shorts, black shoes and sweet little white socks. The only acceptable alternative has traditionally been no socks at all, but black leather is, in fact, a perfect foil for those short day-glo socks in lime green or shocking pink that used to go with Jerry Lee Lewis.

All shoes of this sort are lightweight, and offer no protection from the cold or the wet. And your feet are particularly vulnerable to both. They used to make wool-lined bootees for winter but general opinion has now decided that it's best to leave the job of insulation to your socks, and water is kept out by either a plastic pocket attached to the toe-clip or by an overshoe — a sort of galosh.

In winter you need long socks and, especially if you're wearing some kind of britches, you need them long enough to cover the knee — a hard-working, sensitive and much-neglected joint. Amazingly, the long socks sold in cycle shops are almost always too short, but you can usually find what you're looking for at an establishment catering for climbers.

When winter really cracks the whip, one pair of socks is not enough. The measure of how effectively you cope with the cold is the care you take of your extremities. As the temperature drops, you can begin by slipping a pair of your light summer socks on first, and for the worst of January a pair of 'thermals' from Damart — whose amazing underwear will see off almost all frost — should provide the complete armour. Note though that these should be worn as well and not instead of the others.

The Body: Part One

Below the waist temperature takes second place to comfort. Your thighs are doing a lot of work and can generate quite some heat. For this reason alone shorts are the best things to wear for much of the year. Even in the rain, your legs dry quicker than any material.

For obvious reasons, a thick seam running round the crutch is to be avoided (heavy jeans are often bad for this) and if your shorts are too short the leg can ride up under you, get trapped between seat (yours) and saddle, and cause just as much discomfort. Your waist should always be as unrestricted as possible, as should your thighs and knees. Tight blue denims with a heavy belt and thick raised seams are about the worst thing you can wear on a bicycle. Purpose-built cycling shorts and trousers are designed with seams that run round the outside of the saddle area, and some of them are lined with a pad of chamois leather. They are lovely to wear but completely impractical for anything other than riding. Since they're always made of quick-drying artificial jersey these days, though, and if you can arrange to leave ordinary clothes at work, they are a convenient garment for the commuter journey.

Skirts and dresses can be worn with either an open-frame bike or with a crossbar. On the whole, though, they tend to billow and get caught up in bits of the machine, so better solutions can be found. One that is highly recommended is the culotte which, since it ends somewhere around the knee, could almost have been designed for the cyclist. It must also be said that women on bicycles are liable to be harrassed by the more intelligent car driver, who likes to share his ready wit and enlightened attitude to human relations with anyone he meets. I don't like to suggest that you should allow his existence to affect your actions,

but it is probably illegal to slip a can of Mace into your bottle cage, and the problem will be worse if you wear a dress.

The trouble with any garment that extends below the knee is that it can get caught up in the chain or brakes — though a little care should avoid this — and it always gets oil on the inside right leg. Even those who never, ever, got ink on their fingers at school find this hard to avoid.

The traditional solution to the flapping trouser problem is the clip, a broken circle of springy metal which cuts into your leg, and always lets a flap of trouser sneak out into the chain when you're not looking. The next most common solution is to stuff the ends of your trousers into your socks. Effective, but it can make for an uncomfortably tight lump on your shin. There are better ways.

Take a strip of material about a foot long and sew at each end matching strips of Velcro. This ankle band has the following advantages: it's quick, it's cheap. Because the material can be, say, three inches broad, it works better than any clip. And with embroidery, coloured materials, beadwork or what have you, it allows full rein to your creativity. You could even make matching ones for secret societies. Simple, isn't it. A quickly improvised answer that works for flapping shirts or dresses is to gather up the loose material and clip it with a clothes peg.

Personally, I think the best answer is Plus Twos: britches that fasten just below the knee. Culottes and 'pedal pushers' work just as well. You can get them made in stretch material from cycle sport shops, but you can also buy proper britches, with pockets, fly front, loops etc, and these are ideal. At the moment it looks rather eccentric, but I can see no reason why they shouldn't be elevated to the canon of 'normal' clothing as cycling spreads, and it certainly solves the problem of changing if you want to take your bike for a night out on the town. Climbing shops sell britches, or you can order them, ready made or to measure and specially designed for cyclists, from the Hebden Cord Company in Hebden Bridge, Yorkshire. It could give a whole new lease of life to the design of fancy stockings.

When it gets cold, long johns are a favourite second layer for the lower half, and those made by Damart should see you through most conditions, but, as a half-way-house, or for economy, don't neglect the humble pair of tights. Choose the brand carefully, though, for the height of the crutch is variable, and of crucial importance.

The Body: Part Two

Almost any garment can be pressed into service for the sandwich of layers that protects your top half. What you put in the middle is entirely a matter of personal preference, from old cardigans, to silk shirts. The outer and inner layers are more critical. Next to your skin a natural fibre is essential. Apart from feeling nicer it allows you to sweat healthly, a subject that only becomes indelicate when nylon or something similar is involved.

The general rules are simple: clothing should not be tight around the shoulders, chest or neck. It should not be too loose, since floppy garments can increase your wind resistance by 30 per cent and make pedalling much harder work. And clothing should be long at the back (as trousers, or skirts should be high) to avoid the kidney gap. The small of your back is vulnerable to chill, and as you lean forward it's the place where your defences can most easily be breached.

On balmy days, almost anything will do — even nothing, although you shouldn't forget the chilling effect of a long descent. Bikinis and singlets may feel cool when the sun beats down, but the wind of your passing can fool you into thinking the sun is milder than it is. Burnt shoulders are always nasty, so suntan lotion is essential if you relish the wind in your armpits.

Cycling jerseys may look garish, but they are useful. They can be worn next to the skin, or over a shirt. They stretch, they're long enough to cover your lower back, and they usually have pockets at the back too. This is the most convenient place to store almost anything on your body, from a map to a box of sandwiches.

The main function of a top layer is to allow those underneath to do their job properly. When it's dry but cold the most important thing is to cut the wind. A showerproof nylon or gaberdine jacket is usually best, zipped to allow you to adjust the temperature and brightly coloured to bring you to motorists' attention. With this and a scarf almost all conditions can be faced. They won't actually keep the rain out, but with wool and then cotton underneath you can be surprisingly warm even when wet.

If you've set your heart on being waterproof the problem becomes more complicated. Materials that keep all water out, will also keep all moisture in. You can get just as soaked by your own efforts as by those of the weather. One recommended compromise is a sort of cycling jersey which comes with a waterproof front panel. It's in the front that you need most protection from wind when you're wet (an old and cheaper trick is to stuff a large newspaper up your jumper) and the porous back allows the body to breathe.

For the rich there is a 'miracle' material called Gore Tex which lets moisture out but won't let it in. This is in fact a laminate in which cloth is attached to a layer of a material that was discovered when somebody tried to find out what happened when you stretch the stuff they put on non-stick saucepans. What happened was a net of very fine holes, smaller than molecules of water, so the rain can't get in, and yet larger than molecules of water vapour so moisture can evaporate through it. Gore-Tex does work, although it requires rather careful maintenance and is somewhat stiff and awkward at its present level of development. It is, however, fiendishly expensive.

Capes have been popular for years, but I don't like them. First because they are such awkward things to wear, catching every gust of wind, flapping around and making pedalling such hard work, and secondly because, in town at least, it's the water thrown up from the road which causes most problems and a cape is no defence against that.

It's worth remembering that it doesn't rain all that often. No, really. During the rush hour it only rains a dozen or so times a year in most parts of England. The figures prove it even if memory disagrees.

Hands

Gloves are essential for winter riding. Stuck out in front on the handlebars, your knuckles can be affected by the cold more severely than any other part. Many cyclists also like to have padded leather on their palms for comfort, so the hierarchy of gloves goes like this, in order of worsening weather conditions.

Summer cycling mitts are little flimsies of crochet work whose purpose is to hold a padded leather piece to your palm. They are comfortable, especially on long rides.

In spring or autumn you can either use cycling gloves similar to the summer ones, but with more substantial backing to protect the hand, or the ordinary leather or woollen variety.

In winter or when it's wet (gloves are one item that doesn't work at all once wet), the best solution I know is to buy a pair of ski gloves. These are well padded and waterproof, more flexible than heavy leather motorbike gauntlets, and very effective. When it gets very cold a thin inner glove can be useful, and Damart's thermal range is again an old favourite.

Head

In summer a cotton cap to keep the sun off, in winter a woollen hat or balaclava helmet (people who wear glasses have special needs, see Chapter 7). Training caps are tight fitting and peaked with a handy flap that rolls down over the ears — a most important point — but no different in operation from your common-or-garden bobble cap. Whatever your taste something is essential, for the head is like a magnificent radiator, pouring your body heat out into the air. A tight woollen hat not only keeps the warmth in best, but it has no brims, ostrich feathers or other decorative projections to interfere with the vision out of the corner of your eyes — a vital sense in traffic. Apart from that, your hat is an opportunity to let the full glory of your individuality shine out.

Neck

The neck is one of the places where your defences are most likely to fall apart, hence the usefulness of scarves to bandage over the cracks. However, beware the sad fate of Isadora Duncan, strangled when her bit of chiffon got tangled in a (car) wheel, and always tuck the ends in somewhere. Apart from anything else, it stops the thing unwrapping.

TOOT TOOT

Chapter 9

Accessories

NO bike is ever wheeled out of the shop for the exact price displayed in the window, except possibly the very cheapest special offers. For your £119.99, or whatever, you will certainly get something complete enough to ride, but for the purpose you have in mind there's bound to be something missing — be it pump, or bell or saddlebag, or even just a spanner. This is not entirely the tradesman's hustle for it does allow you to choose what bits and pieces you need to fit the purpose you have in mind. What's the point in paying for a bell you're only going to lose at the back of a cupboard.

For convenience we could use the word accessories for all the things you can add to a basic bike, though they range from near-essentials to fantastical frivolities. The range is wide — it is truly amazing what you can stick, bolt or clip on to such a simple object provided you have the mind and the wallet.

Mudguards

There is something satisfying about the stripped-down purity of a bike with no guards, and for the seconds-conscious racer they represent a significant increase in weight and wind resistance. The rest of us need them, for they're the only practical protection against a wet road. For once there is a clear answer to the best choice.

Metal mudguards, the old standby, are heavy, noisy, dirty, and very strong. They can be used to mount lights and reflectors, they will keep window-cleaners' ladders or sacks of potatoes clear of the wheel, even when old and riddled with rust they can be painted bright colours. When they get bent and awkward in old age, as most mudguards seem to, they can be forced back into a convenient shape. They are, however, the old-fashioned solution. Plastic guards are cheaper, and much weaker, than metal, but they have eliminated most of the other vices of metal and are easy to take on and off. They have a tendency to distort or crack, however, which is when you find they're an awkward shape to fit into a dustbin. These two types have their virtues and *were* perfectly service-able. They have now been completely over-shadowed by light guards made in a material called chromoplastic. Manufactured by a firm called EsGee in Germany, these can apparently be washed, wrung out, tied in a knot and then re-mounted as if nothing has happened. I don't know why you would want to do this, but it's an indication of how indestructible they are. They are perhaps twice as expensive as ordinary plastic, but they last twice as long and give fewer problems. The recom-mended solution — except for window cleaners.

Bells

Once upon a time the bell was the extra you always got with your solid new Raleigh, and it would have the name of the shop emblazoned on it. This practice has rather gone out of favour, perhaps because so many bells seem to give a rasping croak instead of a clear tinkle after only a few months.

The merry ring of the bicycle bell is one of the traditional sounds of English country Arcadia, heralding the approach of policeman, postman or district nurse. The Highway Code says that: 'It's a good idea to fit a bell,' but I think they too are suffering from the national nostalgia. I rather like

bells, but their merry ring is about as much use in a six-lane traffic jam as a polite 'excuse me' in a riot. Bells for style, then, especially if you can find a good one (it's a matter of trial and error) but some other form of audible warning should be relied on. The most useful you have already: your voice. A loud shout will get the attention of most pedestrians and other cyclists, and it works even better if you can add a touch of panic to its tones. This is not too difficult when someone has just stepped off the pavement into your path. Try to give your warning as early as possible, and make it a clear instruction like: 'You in the red jacket, watch out behind.' Most people's reaction to a general cry of 'Hey, you!' is to stop where they are and look in the wrong direction.

Motorists of course are insulated from any direct input to the five senses, except possibly sight, and normally respond only to messages broadcast over their radios. This can be difficult to arrange in an emergency. However the tin roof of a car has many of the characteristics of a kettle drum and a few thumps on this should get their attention. It sounds as if this situation is unlikely to arrive, but it's surprising how often you'll find a car running alongside you, slowly and obliviously pushing you into the gutter. Slow regular banging is the best attention getter. Pitter patter knocks sound too much like the natural noises of a car.

Horns can be fun and decorative too, especially if you can get hold of an old brass model with a big rubber bulb, but like bells they only actually work on quiet roads when a shout does just as well.

Normally, they're drowned in the hubbub of serious traffic. However you can buy a thing called an air horn which is powered by a pressurised cannister. The sound is extraordinary. It's as if an Inter City express has jumped the rails and is coming up the fast lane behind you. It's a weapon of last resort, like a child's tantrum, which guarantees everybody's attention even if you don't get what you want. With one of these fitted to your handlebars (the cannister has to be clipped separately to the down tube) you get a certain feeling of security even when you don't use it, like sleeping with a gun under your pillow.

Pumps

A pump is essential, for punctures are inevitable, and by the same token you have to carry your pump with you everywhere. Usually it's held to the frame by a pair of clips which can be either underneath the crossbar, behind the seat tube or, most commonly, in front of it. However, a pump left on an unattended bike in the city for more than thirty seconds will be blowing up someone else's tyres before you can blink, so, if you usually carry a bag, you might as well keep it in there.

Traditional pumps are cheap, but there's no point in going right to the bottom of the market. For an extra £1 or so, buy a Bluemels alloy pump, not one of the plastic variety, although these can be found in big stores for almost nothing.

There is a trap. There are three types of valve commonly found on bicycle tubes. The Woods is the standard we all know from childhood, but it's rarely found on High Pressure tyres, and never on tubulars. The Woods is opened by the pressure of your pumping, so any connector will operate it. The Shrader valve is the same as that used on cars and requires a special connector. Shrader valves are the hardest of all to inflate through, but they're quite common, especially on flashy looking bikes intended for teenagers. The idea is that you can pop into the local garage and use their air-line, avoiding the draining experience of having to use your arm muscles. This brainwave also brings some of the thrill of Russian Roulette to the humdrum task of inflating your tyres. Although bike tyres are at higher pressure than car tyres, the amount of air contained in that thin tube is tiny. So using an air hose can, at best, burst the tyre. At worst it enables you to explode the whole assembly and shoot yourself in the eye with a piece of spoke.

The most common valve found on 'good' sporty bikes is the Presta. This has a long stem and a little round nut which has to be loosened off by hand before the valve can be used. It too needs a special connector. When buying a spare inner tube remember to specify the valve that fits your pump. One of the most annoying mistakes to make is to have different valves on front and rear wheel, or

on your spare. It's always the one your pump doesn't fit that goes.

Like so much else in bikes, the technology of the pump has stayed much the same — for a couple of generations at least. So much so, the idea was being muttered that some sort of state of perfection had been reached. A very medieval delusion. Over the last five years everything has changed. We have a new generation of pumps. The differences are these: the pumps are frame-fitting, which means that they are held to the bike by the shape of the frame and don't require clips, and they don't use a flexible connector. The advantage of frame fitting is that it's neat and efficient (the brazed on clips always used to bend and break off, the bolted ones scratched the enamel) and it allows a longer barrel which makes pumping easier. The idea of clipping straight on to the valve was originally to allow racing cyclists to cut a few extra seconds off their tyre-changing record, but it also has the advantages of being neat and efficient as a system. The danger is that, unless you hold the pump tightly on to the valve, and keep that hand still, you will damage the valve by the force of your pumping action.

The pump revolution hasn't stopped there. I have a Super Pump (yes it did cost more than three times the price of the others, I admit), which even thinks for you. I have always had trouble with tyre pressure, either blowing them up too hard out of keenness or leaving them too soft out of caution. This pump can be preset to a pressure, and when that pressure's reached, the pump just stops working. Marvellous.

Lights and Warnings

It's the first aim of a cyclist to be conspicuous. As explained elsewhere the most important way of doing this is to ride in a conspicuous manner. Movement catches the eye, particularly if it is deliberate, while the motorist's eye has the peculiar ability to look right through a stationary object — even if it's covered in fluorescent orange stripes. However, you can't have too much of a good thing, and there are various devices to help you stand out.

Lights are not only compulsory at night — their absence is the most common reason for a cyclist falling out with the law — but they are also essential for safety. You have to be insane to ride after dark without them. Unfortunately bicycle lights have never been completely satisfactory. The choice is between dynamo and battery. Once fitted, dynamo lights are cheap to run, obviously, and when you're travelling fast they can be brighter. However, unless you have a very expensive and heavy system incorporating a rechargeable battery, a dynamo driven light goes out when you're moving slowly or stationary — at a junction for instance — and that can be just the time you want to advertise your presence most. Batteries need replacing depressingly often, and can give out at awkward moments, so always carry a spare. They have the advantage that they can be removed easily, so they're safer from theft and they also provide you with a torch.

The purpose of bicycle lights is to make yourself visible. No system is at all adequate for lighting your way. This doesn't matter much in town, but in the country, miles from the nearest lamp standard, the road can easily disappear. If you have a light that can be swivelled, it's best to adjust it so that the beam strikes the verge a couple of feet in front of your wheel. You still won't be able to see the roadway, but you should be able to calculate where it is.

The traditional Ever Ready lights have been the standby for years, despite two serious faults. The first is that the rear light is bolted to the frame and yet it can be dismantled by finger pressure, so, unless you take it apart every time you leave the

OK, squire. I'm warm, I'm dry and someone else is doing all the work. So what are you smirking at?

bike, you're likely to find yourself owning a succession of useless outer casings. The other problem is the tendency of the front light, which is removable, to jump off its mounting and spread itself all over the road with the peculiar dull tinkle of lightweight plastics.

The best battery light I've found is the Wonderlight, which comes from France. This has a simple plastic clip which can be attached to almost any part of the bike, and a flat torch which slides easily in and yet is held firmly. As an added bonus, you can find the torches in French supermarkets in a whole rainbow of colours, so you can even get one to match your bike.

The law insists that you have a rear reflector (most mudguards have one built in) but many people are not content with just one. You can get pedals with built in catseyes, reflector strips, and even dayglo circles that fit on to your spokes. It used to be against the law to have a reflector fitted to any moving part except the pedal, but this has now been changed, and the only objection to reflectors in the spokes, which make you visible from the side as well as front and back, is that they look rather ugly.

Plenty of city riders swear by orange tabards and armbands and these are easy to come by since children often wear them for walking to and from school. It is only an extension of the same basic principle, though. Always wear bright clothing.

Drinks

A bottle cage and bottle often comes in handy, especially since dehydration is a real problem on long rides in summer. The best place though is either on the seat tube or the down tube. Those handlebar mounted clusters with straws sticking up are all very well for hanging out in front of the milk bar, but I don't recommend putting your nose down by the front mudguard and sucking when you're cycling for real.

Knick Knacks

Stickers, decals, personalised name-plates and the like come more under the heading of decoration than accessory but among the other little extras that can be clipped to your bike are mileometers, speedometers and other measuring devices. Speedos seem to me mere toys, borrowed from a motorised world where you need a dial to tell you how you're doing since none of the effort is your own. Mileometers are different. It's always interesting to know how far you've been (and, if you're on a journey of known distance, it tells you how far you've got to go) so long as it doesn't turn into one of those boring obsessions with mileage that take all the fun out of it. There are two main types: the most common works by fixing a little spigot to one of the spokes which knocks a cog for every revolution of the wheel, and the other, which does away with the annoying click, is belt driven. Both are set up so that they're only accurate if fitted to the correct sized wheel, so check before you buy.

There is also a handy little clip manufactured which is mounted on the front forks. It is intended for carrying tennis or squash rackets in a handy, out-of-the-way place, and it works. Less sporty types may like to know it's also a good way to bring home the newspaper.

Chapter 10

Riding in Town

I remember visiting London with a friend who had always lived in Somerset. Just outside the station was a junction where five busy roads converged. As the lights went through their sequence, solid three abreast phalanxes of traffic would power out of the shadow of one city canyon, angle across the wide open spaces of the junction and disappear down another street. Even a Londoner would have to stop to think before crossing, though not for very long. My friend froze. He refused even to try. He could see neither pattern nor logic in the thundering square dance, no reason to predict where the vehicles would go next. He suspected that if he were to take one step off the pavement, the whole circus would turn into a petrol-driven mob and chase him down the side streets. We had to walk for miles before we found a crossing sufficiently simple for him to trust.

As it happened, the experience merely confirmed his suspicion that London was a jungle, and I don't think he's been back since. He was right about city traffic in one way; it is a jungle. But he was wrong in thinking that meant it was merely violent anarchy. Like all jungles, city traffic has its own rules, and the secret of survival is simply to obey them.

The harsh fact for city cyclists is that the acceptable threshold of error is very low. Motorists can drive on the assumption that a graze here or a nudge there is no very serious matter. For a cyclist, any contact is potential disaster. Like any small animal in the jungle a cyclist must do everything possible to avoid trouble, instead of meeting it head on.

To worry the hackneyed jungle analogy to a lingering death, there is one vital difference between the small vulnerable animal and the equally vulnerable cyclist. The animal does all it can to keep from coming to the attention of its predators, the cyclist must do exactly the opposite. Nobody is going to run into you deliberately. The distinction that must be grasped is between being seen and being noticed. So many cyclists have been heard to say in honest bewilderment after an accident: 'But he was looking right at me!' He wasn't. He was looking through you and that's quite a different thing.

A bike trundling along beside the kerb has been dismissed from most motorists minds in the same instant as being seen, but the same cyclist, firmly planted in the middle of the lane, forces the motorist to pay attention. You should always be as considerate to other road users as you can, you should follow the highway code and ride as far on the left as is practical, there's no point in being an aggressive troublemaker. Equally there is no mileage in being diffident.

Already it is apparent that this chapter is going to read like an intemperate attack on motorists, most of whom are no doubt gentle, kind, home-

The sprung-loaded spacer arm seems like a superb idea for keeping cars at a respectable distance, but, even in bright orange, it's not all that conspicuous and one survey showed it made no difference to the leeway bikes were given.

loving people. There's no help for it. In order to ride safely in traffic you have to assume that the motorist is the enemy. You have to assume that if a car driver has a choice of actions, he will choose the most stupid or the most dangerous. Most of the time of course your pessimism will be completely unfounded, but, as someone else once said, eternal vigilance is the price we have to pay.

There are two interdependent strategies for coping with town traffic. One is to avoid it and the other is to learn to live with it. Traffic surveys always underestimate the number of cyclists on the roads because they have this knack of disappearing. Any regular journey, such as to work, should be capable of rerouting down the back ways. It may take weeks of experiment, and several false starts, but there is almost always a way. I once used a route to work that was still being improved two years later when I moved. A favourite little jink, a mere matter of yards over the five-mile journey came about because one day I noticed, as I overtook her, a very old lady on a very old bike with a big wicker basket in front. A half mile further on there she was again, in front of me. A week or so later I came upon her again, but instead of going past I slowed down and followed her and sure enough she led me along a neat little sidestep down an alley that cut off a corner and two sets of traffic lights.

Valves like this are important when working out your personal routes too. It doesn't matter how short they are, a hundred-yard stretch along a canal towpath, an alley, even dismounting and wheeling across a pedestrian precinct. It's not the distance you travel in glorious separation from motor traffic that matters but the fact that the journey contains one gate they cannot pass, and this probably means that the whole route is of no practical use to them, for through journeys anyway.

Leaving rhapsody for the moment and back to the traffic. When you are riding along the main roads the trick is to blend in with the rhythm of the traffic, and watch for the give away signs. You can usually tell if a car is about to make a turn, even if the indicator is not being used. I don't know exactly

what gives it away, a certain hesitancy about positioning in the road perhaps, but the signs are sufficient warning to stay behind if the car slows down, for you could be passing straight into the direction of the turn.

Relative speeds are what matter in traffic, not miles per hour. You need to be travelling at about the same speed as the motorised sector in order to insinuate yourself into the pattern of the road. If they are travelling much faster than you there is no contact and the cars just become an endless stampede whizzing past your ear. If you want to turn right in this sort of situation, swallow your pride and ride on until you come to traffic lights or a crossing, then dismount and do it the humble way.

Surprisingly, this rarely happens in towns. The traffic is usually slow enough for a cyclist to lay claim to a lane when preparing to make a turn or avoid an obstacle, without being guilty of slowing down the traffic too much. In big cities where there is a lot of traffic life is often easier still. The weight of vehicles means that you can obtain the perfect situation — that is, when you are travelling at about 5 mph faster than the stream of cars. It is then possible to thread your way through the cars almost as if they were stationary.

But the rules of caution still apply. Car brakes are quicker acting than a bike's, so always have a hole to slip into if the vehicle ahead should suddenly stop dead. And being noticed is just as important. If you want to move over into an outside lane veer outwards in an exaggerated way several times (making sure that you're not veering into the path of anything), wave your arm right in front of the windscreen and don't move across until you're sure that the driver has recognised your intention and is taking action to allow for it. Above all, keep moving. Movement attracts the eye of motorists just as it does of fishes.

Keep your eyes skinned at all times and don't assume that something isn't there just because you can't see it. A cyclist can see over the tops of most cars, but lorries, coaches and even quite small vans form an impenetrable wall. As always, the principle is to assume the worst, so don't go. This is particularly important when riding exultantly down the gulley between traffic-jammed vehicles. This is not only your moment of triumph, it may be a rare opportunity for some poor pedestrian to cross the road. Always ride as if someone is just about to step out from in front of every stationary bus and lorry. Slow down to a crawl unless you can see positively that there is nobody there. And, while on the subject of buses, don't forget that people tend to get on and off whether it's at a bus stop or not. They may not be paying attention, so it is up to you. The natural assumption of anyone coming across a line of jam-solid vehicles is that all motion has stopped. When you come zipping down the gap, don't let the surprise be mutual.

It is dangerous to ride in the slipstream of any motor vehicle, but it's worse than foolhardy to hitch a ride in the air pocket behind a big truck or coach. If the exigencies of traffic force you to, leave at least a five-yard gap and ride at the side of their stern, not bang in the middle. You're probably going quite fast enough to hurt if you run into them. Hurt you, that is, not anyone else.

Assuming that you are already a paragon of prudence and virtue, insisting on but keeping to your place on the road, making your intentions obvious, always leaving a bolthole, then you can begin working on the finer points of style. There is a game which not only gives a little added spice to any regular journey but also helps develop nothing but good qualities of attitude and bike handling. The idea is simple: to complete the trip with your feet touching the ground the fewest possible number of times, eventually not at all. It's an ideal cycling exercise. Non-competitive, you are the judge, the audience and the entrant, and you have only yourself to cheat. It encourages a calm premeditated approach. And it develops the most energy-effective method of cycling.

It's fairly easy if you have the luck of the lights and are willing to take risks like sailing out into a main road whether you can see the coast is clear or not, but you have only yourself to impress. Since all the energy is provided by their own effort, cyclists tend to be misers of momentum. A motorist will happily squander a credit balance of speed by braking fiercely in the knowledge that he has no personal stake in saving it. You, by contrast, will try to avoid any sudden braking and accelerating because they waste your own sweat.

The secret is in anticipation. Try always to be preparing for what is going to happen in a couple of minutes. As you get to know your route, this means getting into the right lane for a junction or turning two or three hundred yards in advance, watching for traffic lights way ahead so you can time your run and always hit the green, getting the feel of other traffic so you're never stuck behind someone reversing into parking space or trying to turn right into a side street. On every route there will be places where you have to have luck on your side, there will be long straight approaches to the lights when it's simply a matter of bothering to concentrate, and there will be others where only trial and error will show the right speed to slide through a complex system of interlocking lights. In any sequence of lights there are several speeds at which you will always hit the green provided you start at the correct point in the cycle. The faster ones may be beyond your capacity, so slow down for the one you can manage. It will be the fastest way as you'll be able to prove if a motorbike rides through with you, accelerating away from each red light only to stop at the next while you catch up and slide through at your own pace.

You won't want to play this every day, and the first few times will require fiendish concentration and much wobbling at a virtual standstill praying for the lights to change. With practice it becomes second nature to apply the principles of The Game, even when you are not playing, and then a clear round will not be far away. The first time I did it on one particular journey to work, the record then stood at two touches, it wasn't until more than halfway that I realised the record was on. Then I really started trying.

Strangely I've never found any difficulty about keeping to the rules. There was no temptation to run through a yellow light, or slip over the pedestrian crossing when someone was just stepping on to it. Once I've done any route in both directions I never consciously try again, but still

An absolute must for bike-freaks, phone-freaks and, apparently, technical copywriters. Paul Redfern has a radio-telephone equipped tricycle.

you can ride safely and quickly without anxiety.

The frustrations of driving a car in traffic being what they are, it is inevitable that some drivers will try to take it out on cyclists, who not only get to their destination quicker, but pay no Road Fund license or garage bill and can always find somewhere to park. Shout back, by all means, it may do some good, but don't let your own temper fray. The fresh air, the exercise, the sense of being in control of your own destiny are all doing your soul good and anger would only spoil your day. All cyclists though will eventually have the frightening experience of meeting real malevolence when you realise that someone has deliberately tried to run you off the road. Most of the time there is nothing you can do, the culprit is already disappearing into the distance. Sometimes, though, they get caught at lights. Ride up to them, bang on their roofs, shout through their windows, make it clear that you don't accept the role of passive victim, and be prepared for a quick getaway if they show signs of wanting to continue the argument on the pavement with a starting handle.

As confidence and experience develops, the underlying anxiety which riding in traffic brings begins to fade away. It becomes second nature to ride defensively, as if the worst were about to happen, and then you discover it is possible to be in control of your own destiny on the road. But with care you can eliminate almost all risks except the blind hand of fate, you don't have to rely on the skill and responsibility of others for your safety, you can make adequate allowance for their lack of it. Every so often you will do something silly yourself. With luck you will be the only one to notice that you hadn't seen the car coming round the corner or the parking driver about to fling open a door into your face. Just make a mental note to be more careful in future, and keep your concentration up, then fear, the biggest killer of joy, need play no part in your travelling life. And, in the meantime, join any local bike groups and add your might to any campaigns for better facilities for cyclists in town.

The choice between chains and cables is not as one-sided as it looks. Chains are usually stronger,

the clear runs come automatically. And sometimes, when meeting for a time an old route, I've found myself slipping automatically into the old rhythm of changing lanes early, steady at the roundabouts, speed up to get these lights. Such instincts can only be good, and instinctive is what you want them to be. The goal of riding around in town traffic is to find that happy medium between automatic pilot and fiercely self-conscious concentration so that

83

and they certainly resist bolt cutters better, but the cables have the useful quality of being very difficult to saw through with a hacksaw blade, so you make your choice and gamble on the tools the thief is carrying today.

In an ideal world there would be specially designed bike parking facilities at almost every corner. They can be made so as to be effective yet unobtrusive, but very few councils have got round to spending the necessary money — negligible as it is compared to the sums spent on stacking away cars. Those facilities that are provided are often bad for your bike. Those that work by simply gripping the bottom of a wheel, for instance, such as diagonal runnels in concrete blocks, can often result in a buckled rim.

In your own interests you will have locked your bike to some firmly rooted object like a tree or a lamp-post and removed all detachable objects (pumps, lights, etc., are obviously removable, but don't forget that wheels can be prised away by anybody with a spanner handy, so run a long chain through both of them as well as the frame), but you shouldn't ignore the interest of others either. Bikes can easily be tucked away against railing or posts so they don't interfere with others. It's selfish to allow them to get in a pedestrian's way. The blind can easily miss a jutting wheel with their stick and suffer a fall. Every time you lock up your bike, ask yourself if it would be in the way of a blind person, someone pushing a pram or in a wheelchair, or someone relying on a stick. If it would, move it.

For instance, bikes chained to posts or rails at the edge of pavements should be fixed to the traffic side not the people side. Like most good cycling habits, it soon becomes second nature.

What do you do with your bike when you are not riding it? Once upon a time, if an older generation's nostalgia serves us truly, you just propped it against a wall and left it. There are very few towns now where your bike would still be there when you come back.

Short of carrying around several feet of anchor chain and a four-pound padlock there is no known way of making sure that your bike will stay yours for ever. There are, however, rules which will prolong the relationship.

If possible bring the bike in off the street. At home prop it up in the hall if you haven't got a shed or garage (who with a flat has?) but never leave it all night on the street. Two nights in the same place and someone will come back with a pair of boltcutters. Bikes hang very well and a lot of the spare space in small city accommodation is above your head. There are several patent hooks available for storing bikes high up on a wall, but improvisation is easy too. At work, try to persuade your employer to set aside some space for bikes — they can often be squeezed into nooks and crannies where the brass park their cars. If you make a single regular journey the ideal choice is to have two chains, one left permanently at each end. This saves carrying, as really safe, thick chains are depressingly heavy.

Chapter 11

The Open Road

BICYCLES and quiet country lanes bring out the best in each other, like cheese and onion. As a townie you realise just how much you've been missing, particularly through the senses of smell and hearing. There is time to look around.

Take the simple matter of keeping your bike properly adjusted. The only sound it should make is a sweet sewing-machine zinging from the wheels. Anything else should be investigated. With derailleur gears there are two common noises. One is a regular sort of clunking which means that the rear cage is not quite in line with the sprocket, and the other is a more abrasive sound produced when the chain is rubbing on the front cage. Experience, helped sometimes by a quick look down, soon tells you which is which, and a slight adjustment of the gear lever cures the problem. The quiet is like a warm bath, and you can feel your cares draining away into it.

The first requirement for a country ride is a good map, at least ½ inch to a mile. The traditional cycletouring favourites are Bartholomew's because the shading gives a general idea of the terrain, and the scale means that each sheet covers a fair area. I prefer the Ordnance Survey's I: 50,000 series (metricated versions of the old inch to a mile), although the larger scale means that you will have to buy more sheets.

With proper maps and a little care you can make sure that you never, ever, travel on an A road. The speeds of car and bike are roughly comparable in town, but out on the open road there's no contest. With the anguished whine of machinery under stress the traffic howls past your ear inducing a permanent state of hysteria.

B roads are more rideable, not because the cars go any more slowly but because there are usually fewer of them, and the noise of their passing has not blended into a single disorientating sound. It is difficult to avoid B roads entirely, since they are usually the old lines of communication colonised by the car. However, what you're looking for are the tiny, thread-like minor roads that still cover the British countryside like a fine web. Whenever I turn off a main road and the hum sinks behind me, I can feel the peace swallowing me up. If they could put it in a capsule, tranquillizers would be a thing of the past.

If you are used to cycling regularly in town, then forty miles a day in the countryside can be achieved with no hurry or stress. However, even the best adjusted city rider has a tendency to jerky patches of acceleration and freewheeling. To cover the country miles get into a comfortable gear and then leave your legs to go round and round without effort for mile after mile. Try to keep pedalling and after a while the temptation to rest every few minutes will go away.

You need to take more with you when you're riding out in the country. In England, at least, any ride of more than a couple of hours needs something in case it rains, something for the cold, something to keep your head warm, perhaps something to change into after the ride. It's not much less in the way of clothing than you would take on a week's camping holiday. You should also take sufficient tools and spares for all the running repairs you can manage yourself. Ten miles is a long way to push a bike with a puncture and cycle shops are not all that common in sleepy English villages.

There are, it must be admitted, rather more hills to climb out in the country, but so long as you are in no hurry and have a good low gear (derailleurs really come into their own out of town) it is almost always less tiring to ride up rather than walk pushing the bike. Don't think about getting to the top, just concentrate on keeping your feet turning as easily as possible. If it does become a strain, then there is no shame in walking, it can be a pleasant break in the routine.

There are a few particularly rural hazards to watch out for. Mud and dirt on the roads can be a nuisance if you meet them at the bend at the bottom of a hill, but country curves should always be treated with respect, so you shouldn't be travelling too fast anyway.

Dogs are particularly disliked by most cyclists since they often chase bikes barking furiously and snapping at your heels. Sometimes they even attack, in which case get off your bike and hope that your resumption of bipedal status will remind the dog that you are a member of the dominant species. On the whole, though, they are doing no more than escorting you through their territory, usually just the frontage of a garden, and if you keep on going they'll stop at the boundary.

There is one thing you can encounter in the countryside that will be completely alien to all urban cyclists: the dark. Night time in town is a matter of yellow lights, long shadows and deceptive pools of shade. In the country everything just disappears: road, hedges, your companions, the lot. Bicycle lights are next to useless for actually illuminating the way, so you have to travel very slowly, peering anxiously at your front wheel to make sure you are still on the road.

British bicycle campaigners turned green with jealousy when they ventured abroad to meet their European counterparts. There were signs of cycle-consciousness everywhere.

The ad man tries to capture the carefree spirit of cycling in the country, but someone has forgotten the luggage. There's always something to carry.

On the whole I suggest you avoid too much riding in the dark, unless, that is, there is a moon. Travelling a silver road in bright moonlight is one of the great experiences of life. Turn off your front light (the rear should be left on in case something comes up behind you) and just soak up the sight of your own moonshadow flitting along the hedge.

You get plenty of warning if a car is coming because the headlights can be seen flashing above the hedges quite some way away. Switch on all your lights then and stick closely to the side of the road. Country drivers may be few and far between, but their contemptuous familiarity with the lanes seems to make them drive much too fast. At night, especially, when they rely on headlights to give them warning of anything approaching, you may come as quite a shock to them.

For the urban cyclist, riding in the country is usually the icing on the cake. Your bike is firstly a tool for getting around your city environment quickly and cheaply. But anybody who has a bike, and doesn't take it out now and again for a spin

along the open road in the fresh air, is guilty of a terrible self neglect.

Trains and bikes make a natural team. The train is the most energy efficient, least polluting method of long distance transport. The bike is its natural complement, for riding around in the city and filling in the gaps between the permanent way network and the home shops and countryside individuals want to journey to.

Given the limited time for holidays most of us have, the perfect solution is to take the train to the area you want to visit and cycle from the station into the by-ways and backroads. In Britain you can do this for free.

When British Rail experimentally abolished any

With limited time and the dismemberment of the railways, you sometimes need to use a car to get to see the countryside.

charge for carrying bikes in the luggage vans everybody, including the cycling organisations, was surprised by the numbers who took up the offer. This meant extra revenue and, on the whole, they welcomed it. But they also found that many commuters were taking the sensible course of riding to the station, putting the bike on a train,

89

and then riding from the station to work. On no real evidence beyond a few cantankerous letters from professional complainers, they decided this was inconvenient and there are now restrictions on the free carriage of bicycles during rush hours in several metropolitan districts. You can, however, take your bike on the train then if you are willing to pay the old half-fare charge.

The campaign to make all bike transport free continues, but in the meantime the railway planners continue their inability to grasp the advantages of the transport system they run by ordering rolling stock which is designed without any thought for what makes trains useful. For cyclists this has meant the running of trains with either no luggage space at all (how stupid can you get?) or such limited room that bikes can genuinely be said to get in the way.

In effect, cyclists are told that the trains will carry their bikes provided very few of us use the service. This Catch 22 should be treated with the contempt it deserves, and if the point is made often enough the bureaucrats may get it into their heads that railways should be designed to fit in with the needs of their users — not the other way round. After all, water can wear away a stone.

If you are taking your bike by train you should fix on a label giving your destination as well as your name and address. This is only sensible, but if you don't give the destination the guard is entitled to refuse to accept the bike as well. A piece of rope or string to lash the machine so it doesn't fall over is also wise.

Most European train services will carry bikes, but their terms and conditions vary. In France, for instance, the bike has to be consigned to the untender care of the authorities who supervise the loading and unloading, and choose which train it will travel on — often not the same as the one you're using. Always check with the relevant tourist office.

Almost all airlines will accept bikes, and most will add them into your baggage allowance, but each has its own regulations concerning packing, removal of pedals, etc., so check well in advance.

Chapter 12

Accidents and Disasters

A very big and very Scottish reporter was telling me in the pub that he too had been a cyclist. In an earlier, and it must have been less bulky, incarnation he had spent pleasant days hauling himself over the mighty corrugations of his homeland. One day, so his story went, when descending into some glen, a stone had flipped up from under his tyre and knocked the quick-release lever on his front wheel loosening it completely. At the next bump the wheel had dropped out of the forks and rolled away on its own leaving him shooting down hill at about 30 mph only a split second away from the most sudden stop imaginable when his forks ploughed into the tarmac. Nothing but the bike was broken I'm glad to say, and I've always felt that having met someone who had suffered such an unlikely accident I was bound to be spared it myself. All the same I always make sure that my own quick-release levers point backwards and upwards when tight. You can't be too careful.

Accidents will happen, though you can take steps to make sure they are both rare and not too serious. Of all the accidents a cyclist suffers, the most common must be falling off the bike. While never recommended, the act of falling four feet or so when moving at the cyclists' average of, say, 10 — 16 mph is well within the design characteristics of the human body. In other words you may easily scratch and bruise yourself, but you would be unlucky to suffer more serious damage. (Incidentally, the most common reason for shaving your legs is not to cut down wind resistance but to make treatment of grazes easier.) The body may be well adapted to being dropped on the ground at these sort of speeds and distances, but it does not take so well to being shaken around inside a metal box full of bumps and projections, and it is even more at risk when hit by the same metal box travelling at 30 mph or more.

The standard advice is, when you have a choice, fall off rather than hit or be hit. There is some awesome advice in *Richard's Bicycle Book*. If you realise that you can't avoid running into an obstacle at speed, he says, twist the wheel suddenly at right angles to the line of travel. The front of the bike will crumple up, absorbing much momentum, and then you will fall off catastrophically, but less catastrophically than running into the back of a lorry. The theory sounds plausible, and I pass it on because Richard is a source of much wisdom, but I suspect that only an adept of the Higher Degrees would have enough mental control to override their instincts in time.

Deliberately falling off is a more common option than might be supposed in city riding, though. It's your last resort when subjected to the squeeze on a corner. Long vehicles are the worst offenders, though even a Mini can do it when the car driver cuts a corner so that there is no room for even the thinnest cyclist on the crown of a bend. Long wagons and coaches are so designed that very often it is the only way they can negotiate a corner, but this is no consolation to the cyclist who suddenly finds his gap narrowing to nothing. You should never ride alongside a long vehicle. Either overtake briskly, or station yourself at the inside front where the driver can see you. If you are caught, though, and that sickening feeling of seeing a blind wall of metal move unstoppably into your path does happen to us all sometimes, slam on the brakes and topple gently over, making sure of

course that you fall into the pavement.

There are many ways of falling off without any outside agency being involved. Potholes, wet metal road fitments like manholes or cats eyes, piles of wet leaves or mud, or an excess of balance-destroying alcohol, can all steal your bike from underneath. This can be unpleasant, but generally and at reasonable speeds, it does more violence to your temper and self-esteem than to your health. On the whole danger and cars are synonymous, so the simple strategy of avoiding heavy traffic does more than anything else to cut down the risk, but there is more. You can't always avoid mixing it with the motorists, so it is worth examining exactly what sort of accidents the bike is prey to.

Easily the most common is running into something. Bikes usually brake less sharply than other vehicles anyway, but as I've said it can take three times the distance to stop if the rims are wet. However, if you position yourself correctly on the road you should always be able to avoid this. Never sit directly behind a vehicle but always just on the edge, so that if it slows down suddenly you can veer off down the side.

The twin nightmares of every city rider are car doors being opened suddenly in front of them, and the car that turns left directly in front of your nose. You should be scanning a line of parked cars all the time for tell-tale signs: the white staring eyes in the mirror, the shadow in the front seat or the puff from the exhaust that mean the car is occupied, even the door opened a tentative half-inch. These are warnings only. That nervous glance through a door ajar is probably looking out for other cars; if there aren't any, the door will be flung open under your wheel.

Similarly with the sudden left turn right across your front. Cars have indicators, and they also speak a kind of body language. With a bit of experience you can read the subliminal clues — little hesitations about road positioning, slight adjustments in speed — and when these are combined with, say, a flashing trafficator there is fair presumption that the driver is contemplating a turn. It is only a presumption, however, and should never be relied upon. It could be that the indicator switch was mistaken for the windscreen wipers and that the car is shifting from side to side because the driver is trying to find a cough sweet in his back pocket.

Riding through the town you will soon learn that cars position themselves approximately on the road, their lane discipline is uncertain, their sense of the rhythm of the traffic flow crude, when compared to your own developing sense of survival. But the first time you share two lanes with a single vehicle, and it moves into the right hand, flashes the right winker, brakes at a right-hand turn and then, just when you are about to overtake and dismiss it from your mind, accelerates across the road and turns left, still winking right, two inches in front of you. As I say the first time this happens the veins throb in your temples because you think someone has just tried to murder you. Sadly, it probably wasn't true. Whoever let them loose in such an instrument of destruction as a car might be culpable, but the driver just didn't know what he was doing. Opening doors, maverick turns, even the highly unlikely such as a market lorry dumping forty kilos of tomatoes in front of you in a high wind should be allowed for all the time.

Being run into is a much rarer experience, but when it happens it can also be a lot nastier. I have no useful advice for dealing with that tiny number who are actually out to do you harm, except: may you never meet any. If you do, take their vehicle number and the best description you have to the nearest police officer. Make a formal complaint. It's all very well congratulating yourself on your escape, but someone else may not be so lucky.

Most usually you are run into because of an error of judgement by the driver. The long vehicle slicing off the crown of the bend is a classic instance, but the gentle drift into the gutter, or even the back wheel nudge when you're travelling a little faster or slower than was allowed for, are all quite common. They too are easily avoided if you make a habit of the sort of preventive action that gives you the space and the time to compensate for other's mistakes. For instance, try to always ride two to three feet out from the curb (allowing a proper car's width in the lane, of course). This gives you room to take evasive action, avoid potholes and glass, and it makes you more visible.

The rarest accident for a cyclist is one caused by equipment failure. Once in a blue moon a frame breaks, and then usually not catastrophically. It will almost certainly not happen to you. As for the rest, they are not dangerous provided you don't panic. Punctures are common, of course, cables snap quite frequently and chains come off. Just keep the bike on a straight line until you stop and you'll be quite safe. Do keep your bike properly adjusted, though. Loose wheel nuts on the rear, for instance, can send the back wheel askew and jam the tyre against the chain stays which makes a suddenly effective brake. And if you have derailleur gears, make sure they are adjusted so that they cannot be pulled into the spokes by the lever. Both these things can be nasty, but they are also entirely your own fault, and if you haven't understood the last two sentences ask someone who knows to check, or visit a shop, now.

If you do have an accident, remember you will probably be in shock, so have a good sit down, at least, before riding on, and if you still feel shaky after five minutes, chain up the bike and take a bus home. Obviously broken bones or bad cuts should go straight to hospital. Iodine solution is usually best for cuts and grazes, though clean them well first, if you can. If you have bumped your head, particularly if you have a headache during the next day or so, see a doctor. These things come first, but if you can manage it you also need witnesses and a car registration number. If a car fails to stop, and then doesn't report the accident, they have

OVERLEAF: *This manoeuvre in BMX racing is known as being 'radical'. So is any other trick where machinery and limbs assume an unnatural position. It works out surprisingly often.*

broken the law, and the safety of others requires that they be caught. Witnesses, of course, are needed so that you can get compensation.

If reading all this has made you rather depressed perhaps it will be an incentive to concentrate just that little bit more on riding safely. These fears are at the back of every cyclist's mind and if you are not confident that you have taken all steps possible to avoid trouble, they can loom nearer the front each time you have a scare you could have avoided. Apart from anything else, it spoils the fun.

'You're meant to be navigating, Robin.'
'Gee whiz, Batman, there hasn't been a sign to Gotham City for ages.'

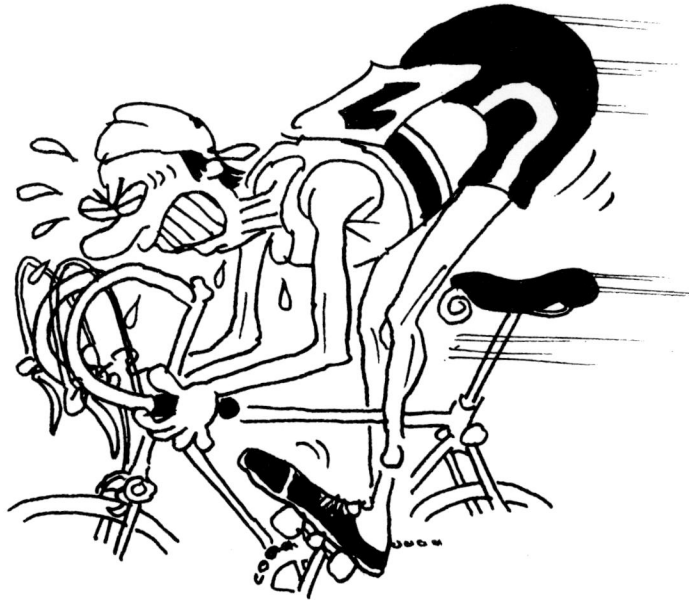

Chapter 13

Competitive Cycling

OR most of us cycling is a means of transport, cheap, quick and enjoyable which we would like to make as pleasant as possible. For others it is a cross upon which they hang until their bodies are drained, their lungs hurt and their time over twenty-five miles has been improved those vital few seconds. Cycle racing is a hard sport which bears no comparison with a friendly competitive sprint up Old Oak Hill on the way to the pub. To race on the roads in Britain you need to be registered with the proper body (The British Cycling Federation controls almost all amateur racing) and that in effect means joining a proper club. If racing does appeal to you, you will need the support and advice of others similarly afflicted, the rest of us can merely offer our sympathy.

This doesn't mean to say that racing cannot be an enjoyable spectator sport. To actually get any idea of the contest you need to visit a track where the whole race can be seen. Such races are essentially a series of specialised sprints under some fancy names, Devil Take The Hindmost, Pursuit, Madison, but although the tactics are rarely subtle the spectacle is exciting.

Road races are a more complex business, with success depending on strategies and alliances as much as on iron legs, but for the spectator it's more usually a matter of a pleasant ride out into the country for a picnic, enlivened every so often by the colourful but almost blink-fast whizz past of a bunch of cyclists on shiny machines. True enthusiasts ride the course at their leisure so that they can make sense of the reports they read in *Cycling* a week afterwards.

The address of the BCF is 70 Brompton Road, London SW3 1EN.

For more specialised tastes there are the various rough ground races. Cyclocross for the purists, Bicycle moto-cross the brash newcomer for those who prefer thrills and spills to simple athleticism.

It is possible to satisfy a desire for the glow of achievement with something more formal than self-esteem without going to the frontiers of the pain barrier. Randonnees have recently been imported from France and there is a growing interest in Britain. These are non-competitive rides of a fixed length which must be completed within specified times — both a minimum and a maximum

are set. If you complete the ride within the rules you not only have the benefit of company on the run but the organisers give a certificate or sometimes a medal for you to stuff away in your drawer. Randonnees can range from a simple 100 km (61.55 miles) jaunt that anybody who rides to work could probably manage with a bit of effort, to the 600 miles plus of the Paris — Brest — Paris; a classic that will bring you awed respect throughout Europe if you can claim to have taken part. In Britain, Randonnees are organised by Audax UK, 188 Runcorn Road, Moore, Warrington.

Incidentally, although you must be affiliated to one of the organising bodies for racing, there's nothing to stop you finding a dozen friends, calling yourself the Velo Club de James Street, or the York Road Wheelers, and getting some of that lovely club riding gear made up for yourselves at one of the specialist suppliers. After all, there are those who say that the best bit about cycle racing is the regalia.

Chapter 14

Basic Maintenance

PROP your bike up and sit down three or four feet away. Examine it carefully for twenty minutes or so, leaning forward a time or two perhaps to give the pedals a reflective twirl. You now know how your bike works. There is no mystery; nothing hidden under the bonnet. The only parts you can't see are several ball-bearing races and, if you have a hub gear, the cogs, pawls and springs in that.

Maintenance of a bike is simply a matter of keeping it clean, keeping it lubricated and keeping it tight. It is all a matter of common sense, including the sense to know when a particular adjustment calls for experience or skill you don't have — then you take it to someone who has. In ascending order of difficulty, the ones that might give you trouble are adjusting the cones and cups in which the ball-bearings run, for too tight can be as bad as too loose; truing a wheel, which can be shown to be simply a matter of patience and logical thought even though I've never managed to make things anything but worse; and mending bent frames. This last should almost always be avoided, unless it's an emergency repair or you know exactly what you are doing, for attacking bicycle tubing with brute strength can weaken the metal in ways which

REMOVING A WHEEL

IT'S OFTEN NECESSARY TO REMOVE A WHEEL TO MEND A PUNCTURE FOR INSTANCE:

UNLESS YOU HAVE QUICK RELEASE HUBS YOU NEED A SPANNER

P.S. MAKE SURE IT FITS THE WHEEL NUT ON YOUR BIKE ➝

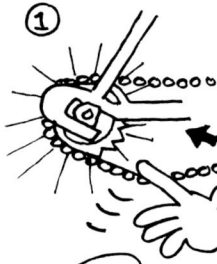

① LOOSEN THE NUTS EACH SIDE AND EASE AXLE OUT OF DROPOUTS

HOLDING HUB GEAR CHAIN DOWNWARDS

② HOLDING DERAILLEUR MECHANISM BACK AT THE FIRST COG

IF THE TYRE IS STILL INFLATED AND THERE IS NO SLACKENING DEVICE YOU MAY HAVE TO LET THE AIR OUT TO GET PAST THE BRAKE BLOCKS. DO NOT REINFLATE TYRE UNTIL WHEEL IS BACK IN POSITION

IT'S ALMOST AS EASY TO REPLACE THE WHEEL SIMPLY REVERSE THE PROCESS... BUT ➝

THE AXLE MUST BE PULLED INTO THE DROPOUTS JUST FAR ENOUGH TO TENSION THE CHAIN EXACTLY.

ALLOW SOME SLACK BUT NO MORE THAN ½ INCH — MOVE AXLE BACK AND FORWARD UNTIL IT'S RIGHT

DERAILLEUR CHAINS ARE AUTOMATICALLY TENSIONED BY THE REAR MECHANISM BUT TRY TO FIT WHEEL AS IT WAS BEFORE

½"
(NO MORE)

THE AXLE MUST BE STRAIGHT ON THE DROPOUT OTHERWISE THE TYRE WILL RUB ON THE STAY

LOOK FROM ABOVE THE TYRE AND CHECK

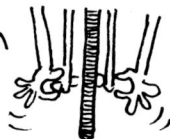

TIGHTEN BOTH NUTS AT THE SAME TIME HOLDING THE WHEEL IN THE CORRECT POSITION

IF THE NUTS ARE LOOSE THE PRESSURE OF PEDALLING WILL SHIFT RIGHT OF AXLE FORWARD AND LEFT SIDE WILL RUB ON THE FRAME.

* LOOSEN NUTS AND READJUST

REPLACING INNER TUBE...

UNSCREW THE HOLDING NUT FROM VALVE STEM

STARTING AT THE OPPOSITE SIDE FROM VALVE PRISE HEAD OUT FROM THE WHEEL RIM WITH FINGERS OR TYRE LEVER

WORK AROUND ONE SIDE OF TYRE IN BOTH DIRECTIONS LIFTING IT OVER THE RIM UNTIL THE VALVE IS REACHED. PUSH VALVE INTO TYRE HARD AND FREE LAST SECTION

PULL THE FREED SIDE OF TYRE BACK OVER RIM INSERT FINGER BETWEEN TYRE & RIM AND WORK VALVE THROUGH HOLE IN RIM AND INTO TYRE

OW! SHARP! BITS!

CHECK RIM TAPE IS IN PLACE INSIDE RIM, AND NO SPOKES ARE PROJECTING THROUGH IT...

PULL OUT OF TYRE

PARTIALLY INFLATE NEW TUBE

PUT VALVE STEM THROUGH HOLE — THEN STUFF REST OF TUBE INTO TYRE WITHOUT STRETCHING RUBBER OR TWISTING VALVE...

TAKE YOUR TIME AT THIS STAGE OTHERWISE YOU'LL BE DOING IT AGAIN SOON.

IF YOU PUNCTURED...

BE CAREFUL!

RUN FINGERS CAREFULLY ROUND INSIDE & OUTSIDE THE TYRE STRETCHING THE RUBBER. YOU ARE LOOKING FOR A BURIED BIT OF GRIT OR GLASS — THE ORIGINAL CULPRIT AND IT WILL DO IT AGAIN IF YOU DON'T REMOVE IT.

ALMOST INVISIBLE

STARTING OPPOSITE THE VALVE ROLL THE TYRE BACK ON TO THE WHEEL. SECTION WITH VALVE SHOULD BE LAST.

PUSH VALVE INTO TYRE HARD AT THE SAME TIME AS SEATING LAST SECTION IN RIM.

DO NOT TRY TO PULL TYRE INTO PLACE BY TIGHTENING VALVE LOCK NUT.

MAKE SURE THE TYRE ISN'T TRAPPED BETWEEN TYRE & RIM — IT WILL PUNCTURE

Pssssssss

101

LUBRICATION

USE LIGHT SPRAY LIKE LPS 1 OR OIL TO KEEP DELICATE MOVING PARTS CLEAN AND OPERATING SMOOTHLY

OIL

USE OIL OR HEAVY SPRAY LIKE LPS 3 FOR CHAIN AND BRAKE PIVOTS...

CABLES: GREASE INSIDE GUIDES OR REMOVE AND RUN THROUGH TALLOW

BRAKE MECHANISM: KEEP CLEAN AND OIL PIVOTS. KEEP ALL LUBRICANTS AWAY FROM BLOCKS AND WHEEL RIMS

BRAKE LEVERS. LPS OR LIGHT OIL PIVOTS

KEEP CLEAN AND USE LPS 1 OR OIL LIGHTLY AND WIPE CAREFULLY

FRONT DERAILLEUR CLEAN WITH LPS 1 OR PARAFFIN RAG AND OIL PIVOTING PARTS

HUB GEAR OIL THROUGH HUB PLATE

CLEANING IS EASIER IF YOU USE AN OLD TOOTHBRUSH

REAR DERAILLEUR CLEAN WITH LPS 1 OR RAG AND OIL COGS & PIVOTS

ALL BEARINGS (HUBS, HEADSET, PEDALS) SHOULD IDEALLY BE DISASSEMBLED AND GREASED SAY ONCE A YEAR BUT REGULAR OILING CAN BE A SUBSTITUTE, ESPECIALLY ON CHEAPER ROBUSTER BIKES. TO OIL HEADSET TURN BIKE UPSIDE DOWN AND DRIBBLE INTO BEARINGS

SOAK FOR 24 HOURS IN PARAFFIN AND SCRUB WITH A NAIL BRUSH

CHAIN: REMOVE EVERY 3 MONTHS. CLEAN IN PARAFFIN, THEN OIL OR LPS. 3. — WIPE OFF SURPLUS

PARAFF

TO REMOVE CHAIN:

HUB GEAR CHAIN:

ROTATE CHAIN UNTIL CONNECTING LINK IS FOUND: PRISE OFF WITH SCREWDRIVER OR PLIERS

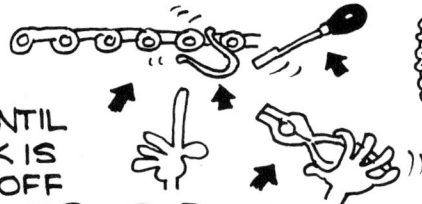

DERAILLEUR CHAIN HAS NO CONNECTING LINK. WITH SPECIAL TOOL DRIVE OUT ONE (RIVET) AND PULL APART

OR PLACE RIVET OVER A NUT AND DRIVE OUT RIVET WITH A PUNCH

PUNCH ➤

NUT ➤

DO NOT PUSH RIVET OUT COMPLETELY: LEAVE IT STUCK IN THE LAST PLATE

← RIVET

OTHERWISE REFITTING IT IS ALMOST IMPOSSIBLE...

CHAIN IS WORN IF IT MOVES MORE THAN ½" SIDE TO SIDE

A DERAILLEUR CHAIN SHOULD BE LONG ENOUGH TO COVER LARGE FRONT TO LARGE BACK YET NOT TOO LONG FOR THE MECHANISM TO 'ROLL UP' THE SLACK OR SMALLER SPROCKETS THE BEST METHOD IS TO COUNT THE NUMBER OF LINKS ON THE OLD CHAIN AND COPY THAT

SEVEN... EIGHT... NINE... TEN... ELEVEN... TWELVE...

103

☞ TIPS: FOR ROUTINE ADJUSTMENTS

BRAKES: CABLES STRETCH ESPECIALLY WHEN NEW

BRAKE BLOCK SHOULD BE AS CLOSE TO THE RIM AS POSSIBLE

SCREW DOWN ADJUSTER AS FAR AS POSSIBLE

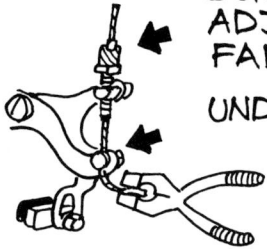

UNDO CLEVIS NUT

WITH PLIERS PULL THROUGH CLEVIS UNTIL JUST TAUGHT. TIGHTEN CLEVIS NUT

THE BRAKE SPRING WILL TRY TO FORCE THE BLOCKS AWAY FROM THE RIMS UNLESS RESTRAINED. THIS IS DIFFICULT WHEN YOU'RE TRYING TO TIGHTEN A NUT <u>AND</u> HOLD THE CABLE

YOU NEED A FRIEND TO HELP — OR A SIMPLE TOOL CALLED A THIRD HAND. THEN LOCKS TIGHT AGAINST THE RIM.

IF YOU USE A THIRD HAND — A PIECE OF THICK CARD BETWEEN BLOCKS AND RIM SHOULD MAKE THE CLEARANCE JUST RIGHT

CENTRE-PULL BRAKES TEND TO BE SELF-CENTERING

SIDE PULLS NEED CENTERING: THE NUT BEHIND THE FORKS OR THE BRAKE STRUT.

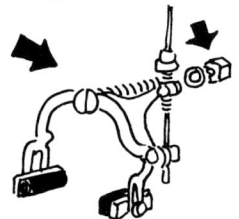

IF THE CHAIN IS THROWN OFF THE SPROCKETS WHEN CHANGING GEAR WITH A DERAILLEUR — THE TRAVEL ADJUSTER COULD BE WRONGLY SET

TIPS FOR ADJUSTMENT: CONTINUED...

ON BOTH FRONT AND REAR CHANGER YOU WILL FIND TWO SCREWS, WHICH SET THE LIMIT OF TRAVEL OF MECHANISM. PUT CHAIN ON SMALLER SPROCKET AND SLACKEN OFF LEVER TIGHTEN SCREWS EXPERIMENTALLY: ONE SHOULD MOVE CHANGER. ADJUST TILL CHAIN SITS COMFORTABLY ON SMALL WHEEL: THE OTHER SCREW WILL GOVERN THE LARGE SPROCKETS (FRONT & REAR) ADJUST EITHER BY EXAMINING MECHANISM TO SEE HOW IT WORKS, OR BY HOLDING LEVER BACK IN TIGHT POSITION AND REPEAT FIRST PROCEDURE

IF GEAR CHANGES SUDDENLY WITHOUT THE LEVER BEING TOUCHED. THE LEVER COULD BE SLIPPING—TIGHTEN FRICTION SCREW

JUDDERRING OR SHUDDERING COULD BE A LOOSE OR WORN HEADSET

LOOSEN LOCKNUT, TIGHTEN BEARING RACE UNTIL JUST FINGER TIGHT. TIGHTEN LOCKNUT AGAIN

HANDLEBARS:

TO ADJUST HANDLEBARS OR IF THEY SLIP LOOSEN NUT **A**

IF THE STEM IS NOT DIRECTLY IN LINE WITH THE FRONT WHEEL

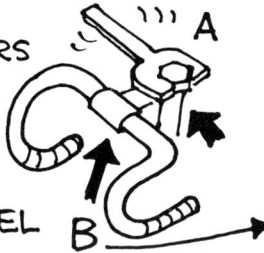

IF YOU WANT BARS HIGHER WORK OUT OF HEAD TUBE BUT LEAVE 2½" OUTSIDE CHROME FOR STRENGTH

LOOSEN NUT **B** TO ROTATE BARS UP AND DOWN FOR A CHANGE OF GRIP

DON'T FORGET TO TIGHTEN THE NUTS AGAIN.

INSTEAD OF NUTS YOU MAY FIND ALLEN KEY FITTINGS: THEY ARE SIMPLY REVERSED NUTS...

THE HEX HOLE IS ON THE BIKE THE SPANNER LOOKS LIKE THIS

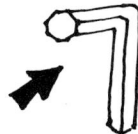

105

are quite unapparent — until the tube fails on you.

You should make a habit of checking over your bike regularly, especially, I'm sorry to say, if it has been left in a public place. Some people's funny bone is tickled by unscrewing vital bits on other people's bikes. At the very least you may find your gears are not as you left them.

Keeping your bike clean, apart from anything else, makes it easier to keep an eye on the state of all the parts. If you allow the dirt to get too bad it will begin to harm the machine. With most of the vital moving parts, cleanliness and lubrication go hand in hand.

Chains should be freed of clogging dirt at least every couple of weeks. Every few months they should be removed and thoroughly cleaned in paraffin. Some people construct complicated paraffin baths for cleaning the chain on the bike but for most purposes a paraffin soaked rag and an old toothbrush will do fine. Remember though that cleaning removes the lubricant, so reapplication of whatever you're using is needed after every cleaning.

I used to favour the heavy spray lubricating distillates, like LPS 3, for the chain. The theory behind them is that they leave a very fine film which doesn't attract so much dirt and other abrasive muck; however, I've found that they wear off very quickly, so I've reverted to bike oil. The crucial moment came in the Brittany countryside when that horrible irregular squeaking, which means dried out links on the chain, began to eat its way into my soul. And the lube spray was empty. And the shops were shut. You often hear that squeaking coming from city bikes, incidentally, and it hurts. It doesn't matter how battered and ingeniously held together with wire and stickers the rest of the bike is, unless the chain runs smoothly, neither will you.

Brakes should be regularly adjusted (see the picture guide, page 104) so that the rubber blocks hit the rim firmly and straight, have only an eighth of an inch clearance, and don't rub the tyre. Some blocks will squeal when new, or if oil has got on to the rim, but this is an irritation not a problem and almost always goes away quickly. Brake blocks

need replacing more often than anything else, but they are very cheap. Make sure, though, if the shoes are only closed at one end that that is the forward facing end, otherwise the first time you try to stop you will spray brake blocks all over the road.

Cables are cheap, too, so replace them as soon as you detect any fraying or kinks. You would be extremely unlucky if both brake cables went at once but keeping an eye on their condition makes doubly sure. The chief danger points are at the nipple end where they are joined to the levers. New cables stretch with use, so you can expect to have to tighten them up within a fortnight of fitting. Cables need lubrication before they are threaded through the casing and a common trick is to run them through a piece of paraffin wax, though oiling will do at a pinch.

Juddering and wobbling can be alarming, but it rarely means anything serious. If either wheel wobbles from side to side on its axle, then the cones need tightening. This requires a special spanner, and if you haven't got one, or are not sure how it's done, take the bike to a shop where the job is a matter of seconds and more often than not a smile will be payment enough. Juddering in the handlebars is usually detected when braking or when riding without hands (a good test for the general trim of the bike anyway). Hold the brakes full on and rock the bike backwards and forwards. If you notice any play in the stem, where the handlebars and forks join the frame, the headset needs attention.

To adjust the headset loosen the locknut, which is at the top, then tighten the bearing cup finger

---

Punctures don't happen all that often, but when they do the difference between a fatalistic smile like his and bitter tears, is as small as a spare tube or a pump that works.

tight, then retighten the locknut. If there is still play in the assembly, the bearings are worn and you will have to take the headset apart. The procedure is commonsensical, but a decent repair manual (see chapter 19) or better still an experienced friend, will make tears and curses less likely. This applies to all work on the ball-bearings which should ideally be regreased every year or so. It must be admitted that many people leave it much longer than that.

If the hub gear trigger is too tight to let you find first gear, or tends to shoot into a sickening free spin when you flick the lever up into third, the cable tension is probably wrong. The adjuster is at the end of the small chain that comes out of the centre of the rear hub, and is simply a small barrel screw. Put the lever into the third position and tighten the barrel until the cable is completely tight.

Most of these mechanical concerns crop up only rarely, but nobody who rides a bike can escape the occasional puncture. This is the bare minimum of expertise. The procedure, and it's simple enough, is exhaustively explained in the rather nice pictures on pages 100-101 but there are a couple of points worth making again. Most punctures are caused by tiny pieces of grit or, in cities, glass. These rarely pierce the tube the instant you run over them, but they embed themselves in the tyre and work through as you ride along. THEY ARE ALMOST ALWAYS STILL HIDDEN IN THE RUBBER WHEN YOU'VE MENDED THE PUNCTURE. Unless you find and remove them you will probably puncture again within a few miles. When you remove the tube fix in your mind the way it came off the tyre. You can find the hole, even without a bowl of water for the classic bubble test, by reinflating and holding the tube close to your cheek to feel the gush of air.

This tells you roughly where in the tyre the culprit is likely to be lurking. Examine it carefully, both by eye and by feel, stretching the rubber to expose the point, and don't give up until you have found what caused the damage or are absolutely sure the tyre is clean. Remember to examine the spokes where they come through the rim. A protruding spoke is the cause of a puncture almost as often as a piece of glass.

Chapter 15

The Paperwork

THE bureaucracy of bike riding is mercifully small. You need no licence, logbook or MOT certificate. So the cycling section of your Home Office file behind the television will be almost bare. It might contain an hire purchase agreement and, if you go camping abroad, an International Carnet, but the one thing that should be there is an insurance certificate.

Motorists need insurance because they are always damaging other people and other people's things. Cyclists, in contrast, are usually the victims and so the cover for the damage they do to others is very cheap and often comes incidentally with membership of a club or as a by-blow of another insurance policy. There is, therefore, no legal objection to you biking without third party insurance but common sense is strongly against it. Members of the Cyclists Touring Club (69 Meadrow, Godalming, Surrey) will be covered as part of their subscription, and third party can be an extra with specialised loss and damage policies such as those run by cycle-dealer chains.

It is possible to ask a company for a specific third party policy, but this is a very expensive way of doing things. Not because premiums are high, but because the actual cost of issuing and administering the insurance is more expensive than the price of the protection.

The only real alternative to one of the cycle schemes is in your household policy. The comprehensive household insurances often include a public liability clause, or you could ask for Third Party for cycling to be added as an extra. It shouldn't cost much but, as with all insurance, make quite sure that you are covered and find out what the exemptions are (racing, for instance, is often specifically excluded).

What cyclists really need insurance against is another crime of which they are disproportionately the victims: theft. Thousands of bicycles are stolen every day, so you have to assume yours could be one of them. If you are very careful, always lock up your machine with a stout chain, and put it indoors whenever possible, you may improve the odds and cut down on casual stealing by joy riding children, but the professionals, with their bolt cutters and vans, can still get you in the end.

I suppose you could always go and take out a personal policy at Lloyds, but there are two standard ways of insuring your bike. The one that is best for you depends on the value of your machine. The cheapest insurance is to add the bike to House Contents insurance (you can get a similar policy for rented flats and bedsits). Not all firms offer this, so check before you insure the stereo, but it is cheap and easy. However, there is always a cut-off on what they will pay out, often as low as £100, so if you are whizzing round town on anything at all special you are going to be left considerably out of pocket.

This is the Cambridge Boat Race crew off to deliver their challenge to Oxford. They are smiling because for the first time they can see where they are going.

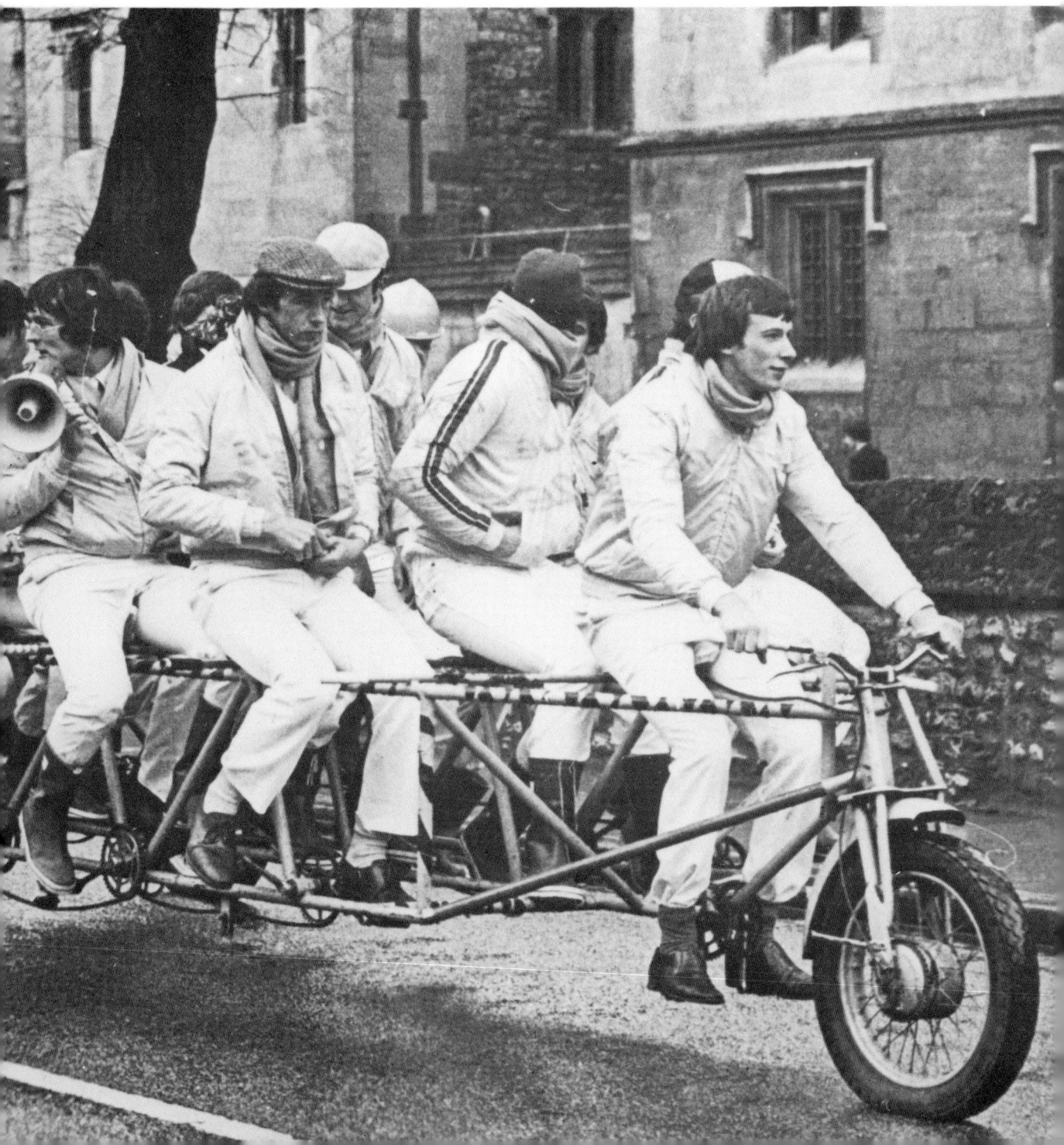

The best insurance is the 'As New' policy specially for cyclists, organised through one of the organisations such as the Cyclists Touring Club which, provided you keep the valuation up to date, will pay the full replacement cost of the machine. This way lies peace of mind, but it is very expensive: about 10 per cent of the value per year. However, I would say that anybody who rides a bike regularly in town for ten years without being robbed of it once has been both careful and very lucky.

To get the CTC insurance you have to join the organisation, which is no bad thing anyway. For around a fiver you get free legal aid and Third Party up to £300,000 and you have access to their touring services. They send you useful sheets of paper with bicycle parts translated into the language of your destination, route maps and general advice. There are also rides and social events organised by the various local groups and, for the organisationally minded, it's a friendly way to tap a considerable pool of maintenance and travelling wisdom. It also, as you've probably gathered, gives off the faint old-fashioned whiff of boy scoutism.

The criticism is justified. Ever since the stormy meeting, early in their 100 years' existence, when the CTC decided not to champion the interests of that eccentric minority, the motorists, the Club has ploughed a magnificent British furrow of decency, baggy shorts, youth-hostelling moderation and surprisingly effective campaigning. With more than 30,000 members they are the most effective lobby for the cyclist in the corridors of power, and the recent young hotheads controversy inside the Club is only going to change the emphasis slowly. So why not take the best of both worlds. Join the CTC for its benefits and its history, and the polite way it rebukes car-minded parliamentarians and councillors, and turn out on the local bike demonstrations with the militants to make your point in public and for the lovely feeling of taking to the road in your hundreds, when not even the wallowing, soft-sprung tourist coaches can ignore you.

Chapter 16

The Law

THE law of the road must be the most broken in the land, and it is also sometimes an ass, but please obey it. If you have ever stood in a bar and heard some sheepskinned fool boast how he drifted his souped-up salesmobile round the corner by the primary school and touched seventy through town past the Old Folks Home, braying: 'But it's all right for me, old chap, I'm quite safe because I know what I'm doing,' you will, I hope, have shuddered. Yet cyclists act like this all the time and can't see why it is wrong.

In most respects the law makes no real distinction between the behaviour of a car on the road and a bicycle, as Phil Carbutt found out when he was stopped for speeding at the very beginning of his attempt to break the Land's End to John O'Groats non-stop record in 1980 (he did it just the same). The bike is defined as 'a carriage within the meaning of the act', and this gives you the right, a vital and important one for all city riders, to occupy and use the space of a lane if that's what you need for sensible manouevering. This is so important, I shall repeat it. You are entitled to ride your bike in any lane and at the speed you judge best and if this slows down the cars behind you, then they will have to wait. However if you were to ride like this just for the fun of giving other road users apoplexy (I don't deny it *can* be fun) you would be provoking a dangerous reaction, a silly thing to do when your victim is in charge of a lethal machine.

The old offence of 'riding furiously' has gone now, though to see someone who has been forced into a gutter trying to catch up with the culprit by the next traffic lights in order to raise the matter, you might not believe it is entirely obsolete, but you are under the same legal obligations as other road users. You mustn't ride dangerously, you must report accidents, you mustn't ride when under the influence of drugs or alcohol, you must be properly lit at night, and you must make your intentions clear with proper signals. All these, and others like them, you will obey irrespective of any fear of being caught. Your health and safety depend on it even more than a car driver's does.

Proper signals, and making sure they are noticed, are vital to the cyclist, even though many motorists seem to treat them as no more than a grudging courtesy. Learn to make them clearly. A common mistake is to stick your arm out straight from the shoulder. You rarely see an experienced cyclist do this: they tend to go for the diagonal gesture, with the arm pointing downwards at about forty-five degrees. This is not only better for your balance, avoiding the arm-wobble-panicky-grab at the handlebars sequence you see too often, but it also has the very real advantage of putting your hand on a level with a car driver's eyes, just where you want it.

Common sense and self interest enforce these laws, but all too many cyclists feel that they are exempt from another category involving such restrictions as traffic lights, one-way streets and pedestrian crossings. Anybody who sneaks across a red light or the wrong way down a one-way street because they can see that it's safe, only has to try and justify this to themselves out loud a couple of times to realise how stupid it is. 'I could have sworn nothing was coming,' is one of the refrains of the casualty departments, and of course you are likely to lose any rights to compensation. But there is another more general reason for sticking strictly to the law.

You owe it to other cyclists to stick to the rules, for the single most important thing that affects the safety of riding in city traffic is predictability. You must be able to assume that other vehicles will do as they are meant to. That cars will halt when coming from a side road into a major road, for instance. The more cyclists who ignore this, the longer it will take to persuade motorists that we have an equal right to be on the roads and that we should be treated like any other vehicle. If you behave like an annoying irrelevancy you tend to get treated like one, which may be a risk you are willing to run personally but is certainly not one you are entitled to wish on to anybody else. Since cyclists get through town at about twice the speed of a motorist and at something like one-fiftieth the cost, it is no wonder that motorists are beginning to feel rather resentful. There's no point in provoking them into open war.

At the moment the position of the cyclist under law is relatively straightforward, but this will probably change as the campaign to get special provision for cyclists meets with success. Although reforms are needed it is too much to hope that the legislators will be able to resist the temptation to muddy the waters. Let your bible be the Highway Code. It comes back to predictability again. Knowing the Code not only tells you what the well-informed road user is likely to expect you to do, but it will also give you an idea of what the motorist ought to be doing in any particular situation. It's a poor starting point for guessing what they actually will do, but it's the only one we've got.

Chapter 17

The Cyclist Militant

CYCLISTS, especially city cyclists, are so used to feeling the underdog out on the roads that it is all too easy to believe there is something natural about the state, the inevitable consequences perhaps of the awesome strength and destructive power of motor vehicles. Not so. In 1906 the CTC survived, only after the matter had reached the High Court, an attempt to extend its brief to cover all tourists. What was meant of course was for the organisation to represent that noisy and eccentric minority who chose to see the countryside sitting on a petrol-powered carriage. Probably very few involved in that ancient dispute could see just how quickly the motor car was going to take over the country, but there were enough even in those early days who realised that the interests of the motorist and the cyclist were not the same. The motorists soon formed their own pressure groups and the CTC, up until then the most powerful transport lobby in the country, has been fighting a defensive action against them ever since.

It was the economic tide of the times, of course, that was responsible for the triumph of the car, not politicking. From Henry Ford up to the first oil crises of the seventies, the car industry has been the pace setter and the flagship of all the western

Members of the MP's cycling club in Parliament Square. They haven't got Hinault's style, maybe, but they have the most exclusive bike rack in Britain, squeezed in between the Gothic crenellations.

economies. The pattern of our working lives, the distribution of goods, the design of our cities and towns, have all revolved around the car. The boom has burst at last. A respect for the environment, more realistic prices for the non-renewable fossil fuels, a respect for our own bodies, have all contributed to break the car's monopoly. It will not pass out of our lives in the foreseeable future — even dinosaurs don't die out that quickly — but there is no reason why it should continue to dominate them.

The car lobbyists are still there, however, and if cyclists and pedestrians wish to reclaim their towns they will have to campaign for it. Cycling is an individualist, unregimented sort of activity, and the sort of people who take most naturally to it probably find the idea of organising very off-putting. All the same there are many levels of involvement, everyone can afford the subscription to their local bike campaigning group — it often means you get discounts at bike shops apart from anything else — it can't hurt to write the odd letter to your Town Hall or MP, and any demonstration of numerical strength is usually so enjoyable you hardly need the excuse of a purpose, especially when the weather is fine.

There are three areas in which cyclists should fight for their interests, and there are also three levels of campaigning. The areas are the law, planning and attitudes, and the levels are the national organisations, local campaigns and the personal.

The law is a complicated and slow process, changing it even more so and only the resources of a centralised organisation are up to the detailed sustained effort required. In Britain this means either the CTC, which has a hundred years' experience in looking after cyclists special interests, or the younger and rather more vigorous organisa-

117

tions whose wider brief is concerned with maintaining the planet as an environment benevolent to human life.

Of more immediate interest to most cyclists are attempts to persuade the planners to take account of cyclists' needs. At its most full-blooded, this means campaigning for an independent system of cyclepaths, special crossings, cycle modes on traffic lights and the rest of the paraphernalia of complete separation between cars and bikes. This is hardly practical, probably not desirable, and most people would settle for a mixed system, with separated lanes on main roads, special provision for cyclists at dangerous intersections and a network of cyclepath link routes to allow the bike rider to plan routes which don't mirror the car network. You can do this at a very local level. For instance why not join with other residents in your street to press the council for some discouragement of through traffic. It's good for children as well so you may get surprising support.

These piecemeal efforts are all of value, but their worth is doubled if they are coordinated. A simple and cheap ploy such as opening a path through a park to cycles can drastically improve

the safety of a whole section of town if well chosen. This is where the local groups such as the London Cycling Campaign, Cyclebag of Bristol, Spokes of Edinburgh and others can be spectacularly successful. But they do need your support.

Local groups are also needed to campaign for proper bike-parking facilities. The provision of somewhere to chain up your bike at the local station can double the numbers who cycle to catch the train almost overnight. And with a bit of push those bleak shopping centres where there's nowhere to sit down, let alone leave your bike, could join the tower blocks on the list of mistakes from which the planners have learnt.

On a purely personal level, write to the council Highways department every time you encounter a pothole in the road. It's surprising how often this brings results and even a cheque in compensation for a buckled wheel if you are firm enough. And ask your employer to provide a secure parking place for bikes. When you are refused, find out who else is cycling to work and then ask once more. Don't feel foolish. The roads are filling up with cyclists again, and the more noise we make the safer and more convenient cycling becomes.

Chapter 18

A Wheeling World

THERE is nothing parochial about the present boom in cycling, except that it has come to us effete westerners as such a surprise. The bike has long been the workhorse of much of the world. The vast armies of cyclists in Peking, where the bicycle bells make the rush hour almost as noisy as our own, are a familiar image. There is a tendency though to ignore the sheer usefulness of the bike. The Ho Chi Minh trail by which the North Vietnamese managed to supply a sustained war against the most advanced, and motorised, army in the world was a bicycle supply line, equivalent in carrying capacity to a fleet of 20,000 heavy duty trucks.

Vietnam was a war and a special, though sadly not too rare case. But the renewed interest in finding and applying technologies appropriate to both task and resources has led to a revival of interest in pedal power all over the world. In America lawn mowers have been designed that look like little pedal cars. In Africa bikes can be hitched up to water pumps to use our most powerful muscles in the most comfortable and efficient way. Policemen, postmen and even ice-cream sellers have gone back to the bike, and, by a magnificent irony, the maintenance crews on some of the giant supertankers who bring the oil across

119

the world to feed the insatiable tanks of the car patrol their decks on tricycles.

At some point the possibilities of using human engine power to move around the hardware of society blurs into the hazy and unlikely wholefood dreams of the new primitivists. But economics has a way of playing these tricks. If you start doing your shopping by bike instead of by car or bus this is not only good for the world's oil reserves but it can also make a perceptible difference to your personal finances. The idea would have seemed laughable when petrol was six shillings a gallon and there was free parking right outside the store.

The load-carrying capacities of a bike are easily underestimated. With a trailer fitted, you can cope with almost anything that you are likely to want to move by car, except possibly a bed or another bike.

For most users, though, the three things most commonly carried are shopping and general impedimenta, clothes and camping equipment for a holiday, and children.

The first principle is to put the weight on the right place, and that means never on your body. Those little musettes the racers wear are all very well if all you need to take with you are a couple of bananas and a spare tyre, but any real weight on the body is not only tiring and uncomfortable, but is far too high above the centre of gravity.

Pack loads as close to the bike as possible and as low as possible. The English have a nostalgic commitment to the principle of the saddlebag, but panniers are better as well as more capacious. A proper pannier frame is well worth the few pounds

Securely strapped in and with a properly designed seat, the biggest danger a child faces on the rear of a bike is being bored to tears by the parental back.

it costs. Not only for properly designed panniers, but as a frame to which those odd shaped bits and pieces one has to carry every so often can be lashed.

There is no limit to the varieties of bike luggage you can buy, and some remarkable things can be improvised out of bits of fabric and plywood, but for safety they should always be firmly fixed to the bike and they should keep the load from moving about. A secondary consideration, though important for short journeys, is how quickly the carrier can be unfixed from the bike. The undoubted winner is the Karrimor range which can be clipped on in seconds. If you just want to take a bag into work with you, the Pletscher frame has a spring clasp which makes life easy and, helped by an octopus clip, is quite secure.

The French and Americans are keen on front panniers for touring, but these can make the steering behave as if the wheel has a mind of its own. One universally approved piece of luggage, if you're going away for a few days, is the handlebar bag. Its carrying capacity is limited, but for maps and money it is conveniently at hand and if you use it like a handbag to keep passports, tickets, and other vital valuables separate from the dirty socks and shirts, it means you can happily leave the bulk of your gear on the bike when shopping or eating, confident that all the real enticements to theft are slung safely over your shoulder.

It is quite safe to carry children on a bike, up to the age of about five at least, but obviously precautions must be taken. Never carry a child except on a seat made for the purpose, even if you have made it yourself. Don't put them on the handlebars or crossbar, and never just sit them on a pannier frame.

Small children can sit on a crossbar seat, where at least your arms enclose them and offer some protection in case the bike should fall over, but the usual position is in a seat over the rear wheel.

Such a seat should have the following characteristics. There should be somewhere for the child to put its feet, and to keep them out of the spokes. The child should be held in tightly, with the minimum of room for wriggling and turning round. There should be a frame or panel at least as high as the shoulder to take the shock if there should be a spill. These precautions sound gloomy, but in fact it's almost unheard of for a child to be injured by the adult failing to keep the bike upright, which is perhaps a sign that being responsible for a child makes one ride with the care that should be natural in every case.

Trailers can easily be adapted to carry children, and provided it is sensibly done this is probably more comfortable for the child as well as being easier for the rider. It also means that younger children can be transported. However, a trailer is very close to the ground, so to make sure that drivers notice that something is attached to the back of the bike, some sort of pennant should be flown. A piece of bamboo or whippy car aerial attached to the back of the bike, and with a streamer of material attached to the top, gives a clear signal at windscreen height which is all the more noticeable because it is unusual.

122

Chapter 19

The Armchair Cyclist

EVEN in its most customised and experimental splendour, there is nothing about the bicycle to equal the artistically fascinating springs of sexual insecurity bound up in the human relationship with the motor car. Bikes seem to belong more on a warm domestic level of moderate passion and moderate life, appropriate to a Lowry painting perhaps but unsuited to the heroic scale. There are signs that this may change. Harry Crews wrote a very American novel about a man who ate a car (he had it cut up into small smooth-sided cubes which he swallowed and then passed on, in case you were wondering). This is obviously symbolic of the role of the car in American life, but as far as I know it has never been done in reality. However, a French enthusiast has eaten a bicycle.

Cycling literature tends to be of the useful rather than the inspiring variety, but there are two classic books of fiction dealing respectively with the social and the mystical aspects. H.G. Wells' *Wheels Of Chance* (Dent, 1896), tells the poignant tale of Mr Hoopdriver, the drapers clerk, who took to the roads of southern England on a bike in search of liberation from drudgery and class. A vain ambition as it turns out but a reminder that the bicycle was indeed a revolutionary force in its time. It gave an

123

unaccustomed freedom to women and, for the first time, a technological invention could be seen quite clearly to have narrowed the gap in freedom and opportunities between ordinary people and the rich.

On a more serious level, Flann O'Brien's *The Third Policeman* (Pan Books, 1974), explores the very real problem of people who ride their bicycles so much they turn into bicycles themselves. The phenomenon of the exchange of atoms is well known, but it was O'Brien who spotted the connection between this and the local postman who couldn't stand up in a pub unless he was leant against the wall. The implications need pondering.

Otherwise most bicycling books have a more limited scope, although there are plenty of them. The list that follows is extremely selective.

The Tour de France, as a sporting event of truly Homeric proportions, has inspired a library of accounts on its own, and a surprising number of them in English. Ralph Hurne's novel, *The Yellow Jersey* (Weidenfeld & Nicolson, 1973), apart from being a good story in its own right, conveys a flavour of the personal endurance required to enter the struggle at all, and Geoffrey Nicholson's *The Great Bike Race* (Pan Books, 1975), centred on the story of the 1976 Tour is an entertaining and accessible guide to the strategy and tactics which keep most of France occupied for three weeks of the year. Apart from anything else, it certainly beats reading about football.

The best first handbook for all amateur cyclists is *Richard's Bicycle Book* by Richard Ballantine (Pan Books, 1975). This is widely prized for its maintenance section which is about the only successful attempt to be both comprehensive and comprehensible.

Even more worth buying, if only because it is so cheap, is the *Reader's Digest Basic Guide To The Maintenance of Bicycles and Mopeds* (Reader's Digest, 1973). In strip form, this will take you through most of the mechanical problems you're likely to feel competent enough to handle, though sometimes the very brief text requires a fair amount of cross checking between what's on the page and what's on the end of your screwdriver. It's especially good for straightforward roadster bikes which are often ignored in more ambitious manuals.

If you really want to know what's going on when you ride your bike, the bible is *Bicycling Science* by Frank Rowland Whitt and David Gordon Wilson (published by the Massachusetts Institute of Technology). This explains, in equations and tables, the various forces that are being balanced by your bike and why you're sweating so much as you ride uphill. The book must be rated difficult for non-scientists, but it is fascinating.

The CTC Route Guide is the first attempt to put their considerable experience in getting about Great Britain, without meeting too many cars and lorries, between hard covers. There are 365 routes given, and, even if you prefer to plan your own day's meander through the lanes, the book is worth it for the cross-country planning it makes possible.

There are many American volumes on cycling, though availability in Britain is somewhat erratic, but the granddaddy of them all is Fred DeLong's *Guide to Bicycles & Bicycling* (Chilton Book Company, Pennsylvania, 1978). This truly does make an effort to cover everything and is packed with marvellous illustrations, including a shot of the author's penknife. It's also the best account of such oddities as infinitely variable gears, oval chainwheels and reclining bicycles. Recommended for every English cyclist who reckons they qualify for the American description 'bike buff'.

Lighter reading is provided by John Woodforde's *The Story Of The Bicycle* (Routledge & Kegan Paul, 1970), a nostalgic but informative trip round the world of boneshakers and Xtraordinarys. In fact the list is endless, with anything from training programmes to screw thread tables available. A firm called Selpress Books (16 Berkeley Street, London, WC2X 6AP) specialises in bike books by mail order, and you can usually find anything you want on their list.

The requirements for bike-route planning are that on the maps you should have good detail, showing every road and track negotiable on a bike, and that the sheet should cover a wide enough area for the eye to keep the overall pattern of the route

Apart from talking to them, the best service you can do a passenger is to make sure they're wrapped up well. Bikes can be cold places if you are not doing any of the pedalling.

in view. In other words, you need to see where you are going.

In the country the Ordnance Survey 1:50,000 series which replaced the old mile to an inch maps are ideal, while Bartholomew's half-inch series gives a bigger area to a sheet and is coloured to give a quicker impression of the topography than the contour lines of the OS. In town things are more difficult. The A-Z series give all the detail needed, but the pages cover such a small area that flipping from page to page can obscure the overall pattern of the route. For those towns which have them, the Geographer's Street Plan series are the best choice. They are printed on large sheets, contain all the detail you need, are coloured for greenery and main routes, and even have a street index.

The true delight of the armchair cyclist, though, lies in settling down with a handful of maps and staring at them until the thick red and blue lines dissolve away and you are left in your imagination with only the faintest uncategorised lanes winding among the contour lines and the woods, to explore on an endless sunny day.

Index